I0100300

INNER HACKER

Praise for *INNER HACKER*

"This idea could change everything."
—Carla Banc. Organizer, TEDxFrankfurt.

"Engaging, uplifting, and perspective-shifting...Ted's superpowers come through loud and clear on stage and in print!"
—Jeff Civillico, CSP, CPAE. Las Vegas headliner, speaker, and philanthropist.

"A hacker's way of thinking can improve your life as much as it does your cybersecurity. Ted makes it approachable and fun."
—Theresa Payton. First female Chief Information Officer of the White House, author, and keynote speaker.

"The best thing you can hack is your own thinking—and Ted shows you how."
—Eli Mezei. Vice President, Warner Brothers Discovery and former Global Head of Content & Information Security, Amazon.

"This is a brave undertaking, brilliantly handled by Ted and the ISE team. *Inner Hacker* unpacks what it means to be a hacker, what it takes, and how to apply it in your own life."
—Casey Ellis. Founder of Bugcrowd and the disclose.io project.

INNER HACKER

A New Way of Thinking

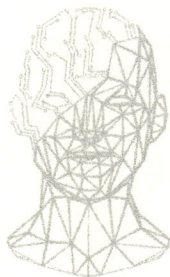

TED HARRINGTON

BLACK
BADGE
PRESS

COPYRIGHT © 2025 TED HARRINGTON
All rights reserved.

INNER HACKER
A New Way of Thinking

FIRST EDITION.

ISBN	979-8-9911365-2-5	*Paperback*
	979-8-9911365-1-8	*Hardback*
	979-8-9911365-3-2	*Ebook*
	979-8-9911365-0-1	*Audiobook*

To Steve,

For being the first to show me how hackers think.
For giving smart people the autonomy to excel at meaningful work.
For inspiring me to challenge convention and think independently.
For encouraging me to keep getting better every day.
But mostly, for being such a great friend.

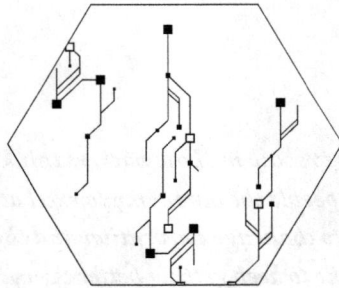

Do not go where the path may lead.

Go instead where there is no path and leave a trail.

—RALPH WALDO EMERSON

CONTENTS

PART III   HACKERS ARE COMMITTED

PART IV   HACKERS ARE CREATIVE

WHY READ THIS BOOK?

Spreadsheets and acrylic epoxy.

What was this hellhole I found myself trapped in?

Under the incessant buzz of harsh overhead lighting, I stared at the crumpled spreadsheet in my hand. *Who prints spreadsheets?* My eyes failed to focus, the numbers blurring into meaningless rows of despair. Another order. Another batch of plastic signs for another homebuilder that didn't care where they came from as long as they showed up on time. I was twenty-two years old, sitting in a gray lifeless cubicle that smelled like stale cheese and industrial carpet glue, wearing a headset that pinched my ears and wondering how this had become my life.

My friends were out in the world doing hero-level shit—

XII · INNER HACKER

scrubbing in for surgery, arguing cases in court, developing lifesaving drugs, climbing their way into executive boardrooms. And there I was, in a soulless box strategizing about ways to convince people that our "premium" signs were better than the other guy's "premium" signs. They weren't. It didn't matter. None of it fucking mattered.

I was good at it, sure. I knew exactly how to position the product and how to outmaneuver competitors. But for what? More revenue? A flimsy industry award? I wasn't making anything or anyone better. I wasn't becoming a better version of myself. I was trapped in an intellectual wasteland, a purgatory of corporate mediocrity where ambition went to die. And yet, that was my life. A life I had no idea how to escape.

Let me back up for a minute and give you some context.

Long before I began my journey into the world of hacking, I was making signs for homebuilders, specializing in interior wayfinding and unit numbers for swanky apartment complexes and high-rises. Homebuilding is a noble and worthy profession. But signage? It felt empty and pointless. If we didn't sell a sign to a builder, someone else would.

I worked hard, but despite all my effort, the world was no different. That disconnect ate at me. I had worked my butt off to get into Georgetown University. I had studied relentlessly to graduate with high marks in the hope that an expensive, elite education would help me change the world. But I was wasting it on toxic pieces of plastic taped to a wall.

Tech had always intrigued me, even as a little kid. It was incredible to see how tech entrepreneurs could use technology to solve problems, and change the world in the process. I knew I wanted to be around people like that—innovating, building, changing the world. I just needed to get out of that dead-end job.

As I learned, though, if you don't have the right experience, it can be hard to find a place in tech.

For several years, I tried (and failed) to break into the field through all of the usual approaches: I applied to roles on job search websites. I networked with friends and family. I even asked for help from strangers on the internet. Unfortunately, doors kept getting slammed in my face. I was making absolutely no progress toward a career change, and I still had to go into my stupid little cubicle every stupid little day to talk to builders about those stupid little signs.

To be fair, that was all happening during the absolute depths of the 2008 recession. Many people were out of work—especially in the homebuilding industry, the hardest-hit corner of the economy. I was lucky to be in a safe harbor during that storm.

That environment shaped me. I learned how to help clients move forward even when their budgets were frozen and their projects were on the brink of bankruptcy. I learned how to spot opportunities outside our usual lane, branching into new geographies and even new industries. And I learned the power of persistence and human connection: When no one was answering emails or returning calls, I kept showing up, literally—at job sites, client offices, and industry events. Over time, that built trust.

Those lessons—along with the tremendous mentorship I received from the company's CEO—still serve me today. I'll be forever grateful for the many blessings I received during that difficult economic period.

Nevertheless, none of that changed the fact that I felt stuck at a financial and emotional dead end—and my pride hurt as much as anything. I wanted to change my life, and I knew that I could do that by changing my career. But over and over again, I was told the same thing.

No. You are not qualified.

Perhaps you've felt that pain before. Maybe you're feeling it right now.

Maybe you too are in a moment of change. You want to take things to a higher level, but you're struggling to make that transition.

Maybe you want to level up your career—to start a company, get a new job, switch fields, get a raise, or get promoted. Maybe you want to level up your company—to enter a new market, find new customers, grow revenue, or raise capital. Or perhaps you want to level up your department—to build consensus for an initiative, get your boss to approve a big budget request, adopt emerging tech, or phase out legacy tech.

It's possible that you haven't even started your professional career yet but are looking to level up your academic life by getting into an elite school, earning a scholarship, or graduating with honors. Or you want to level up your personal life—to raise money for charity, get a favorite politician elected, or find love.

Maybe you simply need a new perspective. A new way of looking at things. A new way of thinking.

Whatever your goal is, you likely know that something beautiful is waiting for you on the other side of the transition.

You may be feeling a swirl of emotions about this moment of change. It is exciting but terrifying. There's potential for something great but also fear of failure and fear of the unknown. The need for change is urgent, but the path is unclear. You know you need to act but are uncertain about what to do or how to do it. What you've done to get where you are doesn't seem like it will get you where you want to go.

Change is disorienting and ridiculously difficult. Change means facing resistance, setbacks, and seemingly insurmountable obstacles. People less qualified than you will get accepted, promoted, or recognized while you are overlooked.

If that's already happening, I know you're frustrated. You wish you were further along than you currently are. You're stuck.

If that sounds like you, rest assured that it sounded like me too.

I've been there.

I know the way out.

There Is a Better Way

After years of struggling to change my profession and continually striking out, I knew the conventional approach just wasn't going to work.

So I changed tactics.

Rather than applying to any more existing job openings, I started to wonder what would happen if I chased opportunities that *didn't exist*.

I'll be the first to admit that it was an absolutely ludicrous line of thinking. Nevertheless, since nothing else was working, I figured, Why not?

Asking that question completely changed my approach. My thinking expanded, and I began to view the situation in a completely new way. That led me to do something pretty unconventional. Instead of chasing recruiters, hiring managers, and job postings, I started chasing investors. Investors are trusted advisors to the companies they fund, so if I could get an investor to recommend me, it would carry weight. Maybe someone could put me up for a role at one of their portfolio companies. Even if there wasn't an official role I could fill, speaking directly with executives might reveal a problem that needed to be solved. And if I was already in the conversation, maybe they'd have me join their company to help solve it.

I pursued that nontraditional path for a while and eventually connected with an investor in a company called NMG Technologies. It was a green tech company with a mission of reducing the amount of water waste in residential irrigation.

The company had already earned some cool wins, including a patent on its tech and independent research proving that it worked. However, it had run into trouble: stagnant sales, founder friction, and unhappy investors. To me, that looked like opportunity.

So I did something bold: I made a big elaborate pitch to key NMG Technologies execs, including both the founder and his CEO. And then I told them to name *me* CEO and give me 20 percent of the company.

Absolutely nothing about my pitch should have worked.

They'd only just met me! I had no tech experience! I didn't know anything about water! I was only twenty-seven years old! *I was telling the CEO to give me his job!*

My mind raced as I awaited their answer. Had I been too bold? Had I been delusional to even suggest it? Everyone else had told me I wasn't qualified for bigger opportunities—had they been right?

Much to my surprise, they agreed to my pitch. I was named CEO and awarded a large stake in the company.

Sitting in my office a few weeks later, I found myself wondering how the *heck* I had gotten there. It certainly hadn't been through the traditional path. I'd deviated from the norm and, as a result, found myself in a beautiful new world.

My time in the role didn't end in traditional success. Eventually, I realized that the product was too expensive to scale and the market didn't really want it anyway. But the experience prepared me for something bigger.

In a moment that changed everything, I was introduced to a guy named Stephen Bono.

Steve is an incredibly talented hacker turned entrepreneur. A few years before we met, he had started a cybersecurity company with a few fellow hackers. The company had gotten off to a great start, but things had since fallen off. He was looking to start over.

Steve and I clicked right away. We discovered we were kindred spirits—same wavelength, same tenacity, same restless creativity, same fondness for weird independent thinking.

In that first conversation, he opened the door to a whole new world for me. The people in his world were brilliant. They were passionate, curious, always probing. The work they did *mattered*. It helped people. They worked hard to improve their skills and expand their thinking.

I was immediately hooked. And when I say immediately, I mean *immediately*. Within two hours of meeting Steve, I knew where I wanted my career to go. It felt like the universe had aligned for us to meet—for that door to open. It was time for me to take another leap.

It wasn't that water tech was wrong for me—it was just that the idea of working in cybersecurity lit me up in a way nothing else ever had. I knew I had to go for it.

Steve and I decided to become business partners, and shortly afterward I resigned from my post as CEO of the green tech company.

That was in late 2011, and we've been building security companies and doing cool things together ever since.

My life has changed wildly. I have the privilege of leading an elite group of ethical hackers. I am surrounded by brilliant people every day. I get to spend time writing books like this one. After years of feeling like my job was pointless, I get to do meaningful work that makes an impact on people all over the planet. It's an amazing feeling.

For a long, long time, I felt like I couldn't change my life. I tried the traditional route and failed. Then I did something wildly, impractically different, and it positioned me for Steve's entrance into my life.

The journey took longer than expected, and I traveled a course far different from any I could have anticipated. Nevertheless, I successfully navigated a stressful period of transition and eventually achieved my goal. I found a different way. I changed my life.

To do that, I first needed to do something big and bold and scary: I needed to *think differently.*

I rejected conventional methods. I got curious about the problem. I experimented with new approaches, especially approaches that bucked the norm. I was persistent and tenacious. I explored creative solutions. I was able to find new ways to achieve my goals.

That's what I want for you, too.

I want you to learn a new way of thinking in order to navigate change and achieve your goals.

I want you to think like a hacker.

What It Means to Think Like a Hacker

I can guess what you're probably thinking.

"But Ted, why would I want to think like a hacker—*aren't hackers bad?*"

No, hackers are not bad.

They're not good, either. Hackers are just hackers. On its own, *hacker* is a neutral term. *Malicious* hackers are bad. *Ethical* hackers are good. Both are hackers.

```
            ┌─────────────────────┐
            │      Neutral        │
            ├─────────────────────┤
            │     Hackers         │
            └──────────┬──────────┘
          ┌────────────┴────────────┐
┌─────────────────┐        ┌─────────────────┐
│      Bad        │        │      Good       │
├─────────────────┤        ├─────────────────┤
│   Malicious     │        │    Ethical      │
│   Attackers     │        │    Hackers      │
└─────────────────┘        └─────────────────┘
```

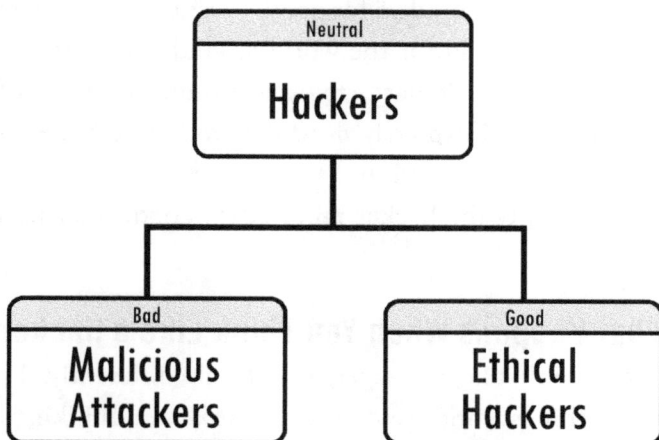

For most people, this line of thinking is a massive paradigm shift.

For decades, we've been force-fed the myth that *hackers = criminals*. News headlines tell us about the terrible things that so-called hackers have done to companies, governments, schools, and hospitals. Cybersecurity marketers commonly misuse the term as well, promising that their tools will combat "hackers."

However, in those contexts, *hackers* means malicious hackers—entities who victimize others.

Most people are unaware that there is an opposing force: *ethical hackers*. Ethical hackers use the same tools, techniques, approaches, and methods as malicious hackers—but rather than to exploit systems, their mission is to *improve* the security of systems.

That's the world I come from.

Ethical hackers gain by helping. Malicious hackers gain by hurting. When I urge you to "think like a hacker," I mean the good kind. I want you to be an independent problem solver who is willing to deviate from norms but committed to behaving ethically. I want you to use the hacker mindset for good. I want you to make things better—for yourself and for the world around you. I do not want you to be malicious, to do harm, to exploit vulnerabilities, or to victimize. (To be clear, I expressly *insist* that you use the ideas in this book for good and not for harm.)

When you apply the hacker mindset for good, amazing things happen.

What Happens When You Think Like a Hacker

When you think like a hacker, you think differently. Hackers explore how things work—and how they *shouldn't*. Thinking differently reveals new pathways that others have overlooked.

Let me state that again, because it is important (in fact, it's the entire premise of this book).

Thinking differently reveals new pathways that others have overlooked.

Those pathways will allow you to navigate change, transform obstacles into opportunities, and achieve your goals.[1]

---

1   Navigating change, turning obstacles into opportunities, and achieving your
     goals are three distinct outcomes. For the sake of brevity and readability, I'll
     often use simplified wording like "achieving your goals" rather than listing
     out all three. Just know that the guidance in this book is broadly applicable
     to whatever change you are trying to navigate, obstacles you are trying to
     overcome, or goals you are trying to achieve.

[What happens when you **think like a hacker**]

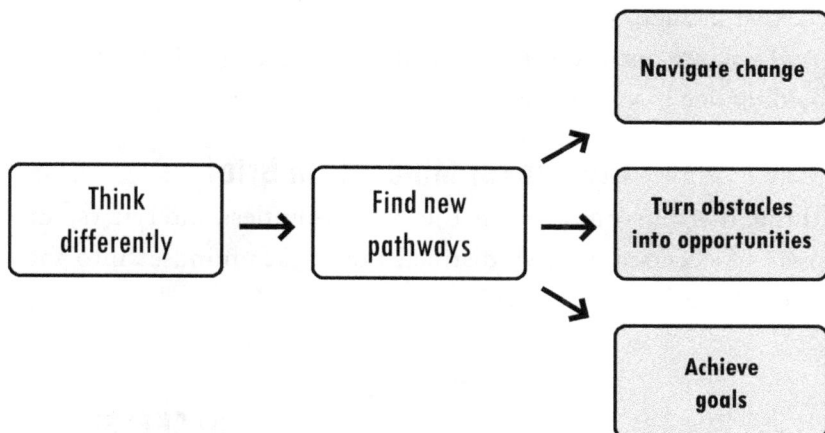

```
┌──────────────┐     ┌──────────────┐            ┌──────────────────┐
│    Think     │ ──► │   Find new   │         ┌─►│  Navigate change │
│ differently  │     │   pathways   │ ──┐     │  └──────────────────┘
└──────────────┘     └──────────────┘   │     │  ┌──────────────────┐
                                        ├──►──┼─►│  Turn obstacles  │
                                        │     │  │ into opportunities│
                                        │     │  └──────────────────┘
                                        │     │  ┌──────────────────┐
                                        └──►──┴─►│     Achieve      │
                                                 │      goals       │
                                                 └──────────────────┘
```

In this book, I'm going to teach you how hackers think and show you how to apply the principles of the hacker mindset to your life. When you do, you'll be able to navigate bigger changes and level up faster. You'll make things better.

This book is not just promising access to achievement. It is promising an *upgrade*—whether you're stuck at the start or already partway to the finish line.

This book is for anyone looking for a new way of thinking. Of course, that includes tech executives who want to run their businesses better and security professionals who want to understand hackers better.

But it is for everyone. It is for *you*.

Whether you are trying to get to a higher level, switching careers, pursuing personal growth, or starting over, this book is a map that will help you navigate the journey ahead.

The hacker mindset is a superpower—one that anyone, anywhere in the world, can apply to any challenge.

That includes you.

If you are open to learning a new paradigm, good news: You're holding one in your hands.

The Hacker Mindset, in Brief

Through hands-on work in the field, countless interviews, and years of observation, I've distilled the hacker mindset into four distinct attributes.

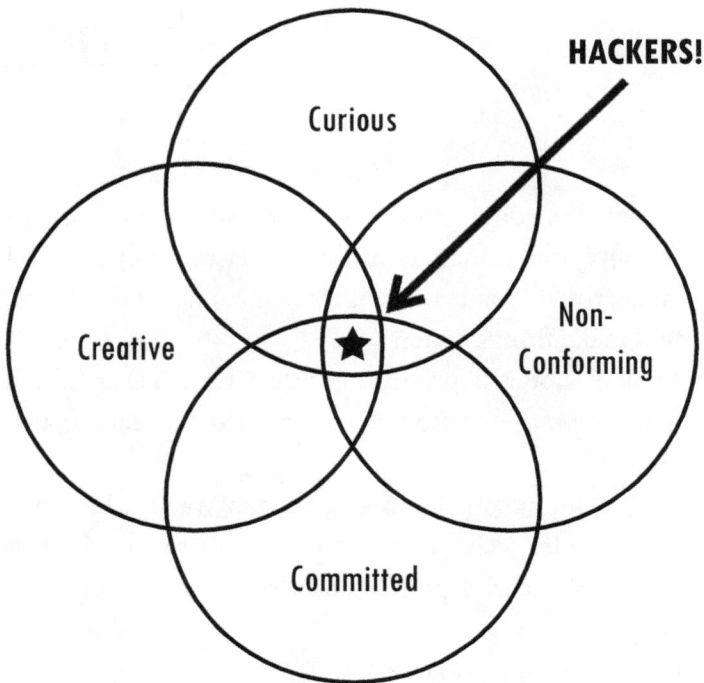

First, hackers are curious. They are inquisitive and have an insatiable thirst for knowledge. They always strive to understand why and how.

Second, hackers are non-conforming. They're unwilling to follow the herd simply because everyone else does. They're willing to deviate from the norm, especially when it takes them into the unknown.

Third, hackers are committed. They're willing to invest time, money, effort, and resources in pursuing their targets.

Finally, hackers are creative. In fact, hackers are among the most creative people I know. They're original. They're innovators. They're constantly discovering new solutions to old problems.

Do you notice anything peculiar about this list of attributes? *None has anything to do with computers.* That's right—the hacker mindset is a *way of thinking*, not a technical skill set.

Like the members of any community, hackers exist on a spectrum. Not every hacker will completely identify with all four traits, and some may identify more strongly with other traits. That's okay. These traits are not intended to paint an absolute picture of every person who exists in that group. Instead, they reflect broad themes that I've uncovered and translated into a mindset that anyone can replicate.

Unleash Your Inner Hacker

You may be wondering whether you should trust me. Good! That is independent thinking—a trait valued by hackers. I'll spare you the boring spiel on my pedigree and credentials and give you the short version instead. I live on the front lines of ethical hacking.[2] Steve

---

2   That said, if you'd like to inspect my bona fides, they're all detailed at
    https://tedharrington.com. As we say in cybersecurity, trust but verify.

and I run a couple of cybersecurity companies: a software company called StartVRM and a professional services company called Independent Security Evaluators (ISE).

ISE was born out of the PhD program at Johns Hopkins University and is powered by an elite team of ethical hackers. Companies hire us to hack their systems—to find (and help fix) the security flaws in their systems before the bad guys find (and exploit) them. Our team has hacked cars, phones, medical devices, password managers, dating apps, Internet-of-Things devices, movie productions, and a whole lot more. You'll read stories about some of those projects in this book.

I also wrote the #1 bestseller *Hackable: How to Do Application Security Right*, which highlights where companies get security right (and where they get it wrong). Then I gave a TED Talk called "Why You Need to Think Like a Hacker," which eventually turned into this book.

Because of my chosen profession, I spend every day with hackers. I attend hacker conventions. I go on vacation with hackers. *Hackers are my friends.*

The point is that I know how hackers think. I'm here to teach you their ways.

I've observed something interesting in my time running cybersecurity companies: All of our best customers hired us because they were going through a moment of transition. Some wanted to enter a new market. Some had recently been hacked and wanted that to never happen again. Some had recently brought in new executives who wanted to improve their approach to security. Some were launching brand-new technology and wanted to understand how it might be hacked—before an attacker hacked it. Whatever the transition, those companies wanted to *improve.* They wanted to *level up.* They wanted to *get better.*

The path to those outcomes was the same for each of them—and it's the same for you: *Think like a hacker.*

Whatever outcome you need to achieve, and whatever moment of transition you find yourself going through, the hacker mindset will help you get there.

Hacking isn't just about computer systems. It's about life. It's about thinking different. It's about *being* different.

There is a hacker inside each of us. For proof, just consider young children. Kids are the epitome of curiosity: always touching, poking, and exploring. They blatantly ignore what they're told, instead testing boundaries and asserting their independence. When they want something, they chase it with relentless focus no matter how many times they are told no. They're funny and wildly imaginative. Simply put, children exhibit all four hacker attributes.

Unfortunately, somewhere along the way, kids grow into adults and squash those tendencies. Compared to children, adults tend to be less curious, less non-conforming, less creative, and yes—even less committed.

All adults were once children, which reveals a critically important truth: *You already possess those traits.* You just need to let them out.

My mission is to help you find and unleash your inner hacker.

If you're stuck, your inner hacker makes the impossible possible. If you're already in motion, it takes you further, faster.

Your inner hacker is your guide to a new perspective, new way of thinking, and new way of achieving. It will help you get through this moment of change, and it will ferry you to the wonderful outcomes waiting on the other side.

Let's get started.

PART I

HACKERS ARE CURIOUS

CHAPTER 1

ASK "WHY?"

Deeper understanding is the first step to finding new pathways.

"**B**ut Mom, *why?*"

If you've ever been around a curious kid, you've heard that question. You've also heard the "why" after it...and the one after that...and the one after that.

TJ was the definition of a curious kid. From his early days, he was curious about everything, always wanting to understand why.

One year, TJ begged for a computer for Christmas. His parents told him no. He was too young. No, it was too expensive. No, it would distract him from his schoolwork. Still, he persisted. For almost a year, TJ asked, asked, and asked again. Every time he was told no, he asked, Why not? When he got an answer, he asked about that, too.

Eventually, his parents relented. On Christmas morning, TJ was ecstatic to see a large box under the tree. He knew it could be only one thing: a computer.

Shrieking with excitement, he asked his parents whether he could take it to his room right away.

"Of course!" they said. After all, who can resist a child's joy on Christmas?

Later that day, TJ's parents knocked on his bedroom door to see whether he liked his new computer.

What they saw horrified them.

The computer was in millions of pieces all over the room.

Unlike most kids, who would have set up the computer to start playing on it as intended, the first thing TJ had done was take it apart. Piece by piece, screw by screw, he had disassembled the entire thing. He wanted to see the guts. He wanted to see how it worked. He wanted to understand *why* it worked that way.

That burning curiosity eventually led TJ to a career in ethical hacking. I am lucky to count TJ as one of the hackers who works at Independent Security Evaluators (ISE). When he told me his Christmas computer story, I laughed—but I wasn't surprised. TJ, like most hackers, is always asking why.

During a recent project, TJ got curious about a hacking tool called the Flipper Zero, an inexpensive device with some impressive capabilities. Think of it like a universal remote control for the digital world. It can capture and replay wireless signals from devices like garage doors, key fobs, access cards, and even some smart home systems. By listening to how those devices communicate, the Flipper Zero helps ethical hackers explore how systems respond to unauthorized signals and assess just how secure the systems truly are.

TJ experimented with devices around his house. It turned out that he could use the tool to intercept the signal between his TV and its remote control. He then tested out that discovery in the most hacker way possible: by pranking his girlfriend. Whenever she changed the channel, he secretly changed it back. When she turned up the volume, he secretly turned it down. She was bewildered; he thought it was hilarious. (She laughs about it now, although she definitely did *not* at first!)

Things got more serious when he started poking around in his car. He discovered that just as he could intercept the signal between his TV and its remote, so too could he intercept the signal between his vehicle and its key fob. Using just the Flipper Zero, he could unlock the vehicle. He could trigger the panic alarm. He could start the ignition. And that kind of control wasn't limited to his own car: He could interact with *any* car that used similar tech. That turned out to be a very important finding.

TJ would go on to present his research at one of the most prominent security conferences in the world: RSA Conference. At the time, TJ was a mere twenty-nine years old, just beginning what is sure to be a rewarding and impactful career in hacking.

And it all started with his obsession with asking why.

That's what hackers do—they ask why. At their core, hackers are explorers. Through persistent, curious exploration, they eventually find ways to make systems behave in unintended ways.

That's what you'll want to do, too.

Ask why until you find a flaw, loophole, shortcut, or other unexpected result. Then use what you've found to navigate change, turn obstacles into opportunities, and achieve your goals.

Observing This Mindset in the Real World

Rachael was excited to start her new job. She'd just left a toxic workplace, and the culture at this new company seemed promising. She was going to make more money. Plus, she'd be working among hackers, which would be an exciting new experience.

Then one day shortly before her start date, her phone rang. It was the head of human resources (HR), who got right to the point.

"We're going to shut down the office for two weeks. Given everything going on with the virus, we're moving fully remote."

Then came a pivotal moment.

"Rather than starting on Monday, would you prefer to start in two weeks, when our office opens again?"

Fortunately for Rachael, she had four things working in her favor in that moment. First, she had taken the call on speakerphone. Second, her mom (who is brilliant, by the way) happened to be in the room to overhear the conversation. Third, Rachael saw her mom emphatically—and I mean *emphatically*—waving her hands, giving Rachael the universal signal for "No! Absolutely do not do that!" Fourth, Rachael has good instincts.

"It's fine," Rachael said. "I'll start on Monday as planned. Thank you, though!"

That turned out to be a crucial choice, because the mystery virus turned out to be the global pandemic known as COVID-19. The office was closed for much, much longer than two weeks. Because the job that Rachael was about to start involved running events—and live events had suddenly come to a screeching halt—she might never have started at all if she had delayed her start date.

I know that because the company she joined was my company ISE. ISE runs IoT Village, a hacking experience that travels to conferences across America (and beyond).[3] It focuses on security in the Internet-of-Things (IoT) industry and offers talks, interactive labs, contests, and other hands-on learning experiences. It's not a commercial venture; rather, it's a way for us to contribute to the hacker community.[4] Given that IoT Village is not our core business and that all events were halted indefinitely, I'm pretty confident we would have eliminated the role responsible for managing it—Rachael's role—if no one had started yet.

We are just as fortunate as Rachael that she said yes that day.

So there she was, in this new job, responsible for events that couldn't happen. What was she to do?

First, she examined the way that ISE had run events up to that point. Even if events couldn't happen yet, she could provide immediate value by finding areas for improvement.

She started by asking why. Why run events at all? The company delivers ethical hacking services—it's not an events company—so why put effort into something so different? What goals did we want to accomplish in holding events, and why did we want to accomplish them? And then, given those goals, why did we run only certain kinds of events at certain kinds of venues for certain audiences? Why did we invest a certain amount of resources in running them? Why not more? Why not less?

Once that "project" ended, she had a deeper understanding of both how and why we run events. However, it seemed she had little

---

3   https://iotvillage.org.

4   This is true, but I'd be lying if I said that this community service didn't benefit our business at ISE. It enables us to find elite talent, network with the brightest minds in the field, and spotlight our research—and sometimes we even get customers out of it. However, that's all a byproduct of serving the community, not the main point.

left to do. Knowing how to improve our events wouldn't change the fact that events had been stopped indefinitely.

So Rachael asked another very important set of questions: Why did we run our events *the way* we did? Had we considered changing the format? Why or why not?

Soon, a possible path began to emerge. We had been running our events in person, but why not run them online? If people couldn't come to us, why not go to them?

Over the weeks that followed, she researched everything there was to know about running virtual events: What were the main platforms in use? Why were they the preferred options? Where did our audience already spend time online? Was there a way to deliver a program through one of those venues?

After many weeks of exploration, experimentation, trial and error, brainstorming, rethinking, building, and rebuilding, we launched the first-ever virtual version of IoT Village. It was a major breakthrough for the hacker community. We ran it entirely online and made it available to everyone, everywhere in the world, for free. People had access to things that would have normally been behind a paywall: groundbreaking research, world-class experts, guided hacking activities, networking opportunities, and prizes. Although we had gone remote and made the event free, maintaining the high quality of our in-person events was important to us. It was also important to preserve the chill, authentic vibe—to deliver the full value that attendees had come to expect.

The strategic choice to run virtual events despite the chaos of a worldwide pandemic turned out to be a very good one. We reached hackers from more than 50 countries, many of whom had never been able to attend our events before because of the logistical impracticalities of international travel. Today, IoT Village reaches an audience of over 100,000 people every year and is one of the cornerstone experiences at major hacking conferences such as DEF CON and RSA Conference. Some people tell us that IoT Village is the reason they attend those conferences at all.

Rachael herself has grown profoundly, from the unproven new hire to the person running all of our marketing. She has been instrumental in helping this book become a reality and, as of this writing, is nearing the completion of her PhD.

Rachael's story is as much about asking why not as it is about asking why. Her exploration of those intertwining questions started as a practical and personal matter: She was excited about the new job and wanted to keep it from disappearing. However, the true lesson lies in the way in which she applied the hacker mindset. She was told that something was impossible, and she refused to accept it. She found a different way to achieve her goals. She helped us change the way we thought about events, and beautiful things happened as a result.

That's the power of asking why. It leads you to deeper understanding. Once you've arrived at that deeper understanding, you see what to do next and why it matters. You discover new and better pathways.

How to Apply This to Your Life

Asking why is as straightforward as it sounds: Wherever you can, literally ask why. What follows are some ways to apply that concept.

A quick note: This book is packed with tactics for you to implement—but you don't have to try them all right now. Some, you might explore immediately; others, you might revisit later, and that's totally fine. The key is to experiment with them at *some* point. Ideas are only as good as the action we take to implement them. So whenever the time is right, make sure to put these ideas to work.

To make that easier for you, I've created worksheets, templates,

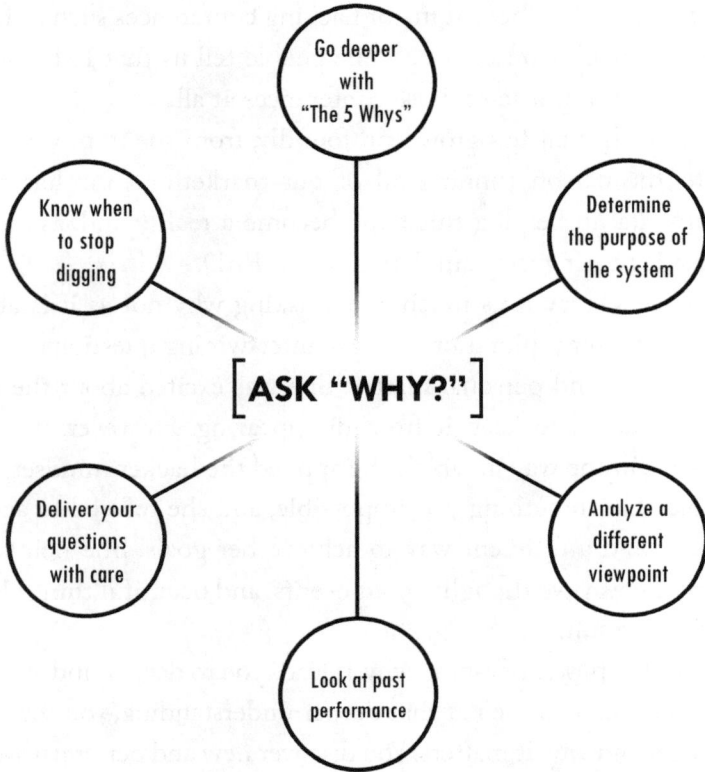

and exercises to supplement many of the tactics you're about to learn. They are summarized in the appendix at the end of the book, and you can download them at https://tedharrington.com/more.

TACTIC #1 Go deeper with "The 5 Whys."

Hackers seek a deep understanding of the systems they are exploring. Obtaining a deep understanding requires them to ask a lot of questions, especially probing questions that get to the heart of how a system is built and why it works the way it does.

To achieve any goal, you need to deeply understand yourself, too.

That involves asking a lot of questions that go beyond the surface level. A good way to do that is through "The 5 Whys," an exercise that therapists and performance coaches use to help their clients get to the heart of what matters to them.

It's as difficult to do as it is straightforward to describe: Simply ask yourself five consecutive "why" questions. Start with a topic and ask why; come up with an answer, and then ask why about that, too. Repeat the process for each subsequent answer until you've done it five times.

Let me illustrate with an exploration of my career choice.

1. *Why do I want to commit my life to ethical hacking?*
   Because it is a noble profession. We do meaningful work, and I get to surround myself with brilliant people.

2. *Why does doing meaningful work surrounded by brilliant people matter?*
   Because I want to continuously grow and ensure that my efforts help other people.

3. *Why does growing and helping others matter?*
   Because I want to make sure that I become the most capable version of myself and leave the biggest mark that I can.

4. *Why does maximizing my potential and impact matter?*
   Because I want my life to matter.

5. *Why is it important to live a life that matters?*
   Because I've received so many blessings to get to be the person I am, living the life I get to live, in the time and place I get to experience all of this. I want to honor those gifts. A life well lived is a life of gratitude.

See how much deeper the fifth answer is than the first one?

Because I've done this exercise, I can see that my career isn't about money or awards or customers. It's about a heck of a lot more. It's about purpose, rooted in the core of who I am. Once I understood that, I could more easily decide where to invest my efforts. Take this book, for example. Writing a book is brutally hard to do, but when I considered it in the context of gratitude—as an act of service—it actually became a pretty *easy* thing to do. (Well, it's still pretty damn hard to write a book, but that awareness made prioritizing it easier for me.)

Most people don't ask questions after the first why because most people are content with having a surface-level understanding. Those with the hacker mindset, however, are not.

TACTIC #2 Determine the purpose of the system.

The first step in the hacking process is developing an understanding of the target system, including an understanding of *why* the system exists and *why* it was built the way it was built. What business problem is the system meant to solve? Why did it need to be created? Were there existing solutions that didn't work? If so, why didn't they work? Why would someone want to use the system instead of a competing one?

Understanding why a system exists will help you figure out where to look for flawed assumptions or poor implementations. One way to uncover those assumptions is to list what's considered "standard," and ask the same question about each item on your list: Why?

There will be certain people involved. *Why?*

You'll have to do certain steps in a certain order. *Why?*

That's just how it's done. *Why?*

At first, this level of questioning might feel unnecessary. People tend to think they've gotten things figured out quickly. There's no judgment in that assumption—but there *is* opportunity. If other people don't ask why when *you* do, you'll be the one to find the overlooked shortcuts, loopholes, or flawed assumptions that could lead to breakthroughs.

Think of it mathematically. Most of the time, when you ask why, the answer will be the one that you expected. Let's imagine that the chance of that is extremely high—say, 97 percent. That might suggest that you shouldn't even bother asking the question; after all, pretty much all of the time, you'll find you already knew the answer. However, hackers would likely draw a different conclusion: 3 percent of the time, your expectation will be wrong. You might realize that something is being overlooked—something that could lead to a better way that hasn't been considered before. That is an exciting possibility, and it's worth pursuing.

TACTIC #3 Analyze a different viewpoint.

The exploitable security vulnerabilities in a system often stem from flaws in its developers' thought process. To find those vulnerabilities, hackers need to consider things from the developers' perspective. They need to understand those developers, including how they think and why they think that way. Then, armed with that understanding, they can look for flaws or incorrect assumptions in that thinking.

Here's how you can take action on that idea. Pick a subject—someone whose perspective is important to you and different from your own.

First, analyze your subject's goals. What do they want to achieve? *Why* do they want to achieve it?

Second, analyze their constraints. What limitations might your subject be facing? Consider real constraints (such as a lack of money) and perceived constraints (such as the feeling of being unqualified). *Why* might those limitations exist?

Third, map out their thought process. Consider how your subject approaches problem-solving and how their role, expertise, or worldview might affect that approach. *Why* do they follow that particular thought process?

You can accomplish all three steps by observing your subject, reading about them, or interviewing them (if you have access to them).

Analyzing someone else's viewpoint can give you valuable insights into what drives their behavior and thought patterns. Sometimes the process will confirm what you already suspected. For example, maybe you believe your boss cares more about hitting her key performance metrics than encouraging your professional growth. If your analysis supports that theory, you can begin to frame your own goals in a way that aligns with those metrics, increasing your chance of getting support.

Other times, you'll uncover something unexpected. Maybe you've always assumed your boss is just a jerk. However, after analyzing his perspective, you realize his behavior isn't about you at all. Instead, he's under pressure from his own boss, forced to make choices that conflict with his values, and is unfairly taking his frustration out on others. With that insight, you can navigate his moods more strategically and position your work as a solution to his problems, making yourself indispensable and accelerating your own path forward.

Understanding what drives people—and *why*—helps you determine how to interact with them, influence them, and align your actions with their perspective to get what you need.

TACTIC #4 Look at past performance.

If you've ever worked with a financial advisor, you've probably been cautioned that "past results do not guarantee future outcomes." And yet, in the same breath, they'll show you historical market data in order to support an investment strategy. Financial advisors literally use past results to predict future outcomes. That might seem contradictory, but they do it because it's effective. Analyzing yesterday helps us uncover insights about tomorrow.

Hackers live with that contradiction, too: They study previous successes and failures, examine what worked and what didn't, and seek to understand why. For example, they might examine an attack sequence that didn't work and explore why it went wrong. What were they missing? What about the system caused the sequence to fail? Could they bypass whatever got in the way? Then they'd use those insights to inform their subsequent strategies and tactics.

This endless cycle of learning and exploring is how hackers win in the long term. It's how you'll win too. Carefully examine the ways others have achieved the goal you're pursuing. Which tactics succeeded, and which failed? Why did those tactics work or not work? Consider the things you've tried so far. Why did some tactics fail? Why did others work? What can you glean from the historical results that could inform what you should do next?

It's true that what worked in the past is not guaranteed to work in the future (although in many cases, it will). But to look forward, you must first look backward. When you look backward, you must ask why. The answer will guide you toward what you should do next.

TACTIC #5 Deliver your questions with care.

Ethical hackers tend to be highly empathetic. They care about other people. That means they are considerate of not only what people say but also how they say it. That mindset is equally important when you're questioning someone else's decision or reasoning. You need to consider how that person might perceive what you say and how it might make them feel. Asking nuanced questions like *why* requires careful attention to your tone, body language, and word choice; otherwise, regardless of your intentions, your curiosity could feel like an affront to that person's decisions or reasoning.

Sometimes people receive the question as a judgment, an attack on their competence, or a signal of distrust. None of that lands well. For example, "Why did you do it that way?" might be heard as "What's wrong with you?" even though that's not what you meant. But as a mentor once told me, communication isn't what you say. It's what they hear.

If your question is received poorly, the listener might shut down, preventing you from getting the deeper understanding you're seeking. There are a few techniques that can help you avoid that and ensure your question comes across as curious, not critical.

One option is to try rephrasing the question to focus on the *process* rather than the *person*. For example, instead of "Why did you do that?" try asking "What led to this decision?" That shift in phrasing steers the tone away from confrontation and toward curiosity. It signals that you're trying to understand what happened, not assign blame.

Alternatively, try removing the word "why" altogether. For example, instead of "Why did you design it this way?" say "Can you walk me through the reasoning behind this design?"

Another option is to use collaborative phrasing. For example, instead of "Why did you choose this approach?" say "I'm curious about this approach—how did you arrive at it?"

Lastly, try pairing your question with empathy. For example, begin your question by conveying understanding of another viewpoint. Try wording like "This looks like it solves a lot of problems. Why did you choose this solution over other options?"

Having considered your word choice, you'll want to think about nonverbal communication. First, consider your tone of voice. Make

sure it matches your intent—calm, curious, confident, or warm. *Smile.*
The suggestion sounds silly, but it really works. Smile even if the other
person can't see you—if you're on a phone call, for example. Smiling
softens our demeanor and causes us to subconsciously make our tone
approachable.

Next, consider your body language. Experts in body language
suggest adopting a few small habits. For example, make eye contact (without making the other person feel like you're staring them
down). Use gentle gestures (rather than sharp, abrupt motions that
could come across as accusatory), and maintain an open posture
(that is, relax your shoulders and avoid crossing your arms). Nod
while listening.

Lastly, mind your physical space. Stay close to the other person,
but not too close, and try to match their energy.

By carefully considering your delivery, you can unlock the full
power of asking why without unintentionally triggering defensiveness.

TACTIC #6 Know when to stop digging.

Hackers are relentlessly curious. They don't just accept things at
face value. They dig deeper, peeling back the layers of a system to
understand its inner workings. This curiosity often leads them to
breakthrough discoveries, but it also comes with a risk: chasing the
wrong path too far. When you do that, your quest for understanding
becomes a tragic waste of time, effort, and energy. The best hackers
know when to keep digging and when to step back.

A hacker might chase a vulnerability after spotting a clue—
unusual behavior, an error message, or an unexpected response. If the
hacker uncovers a deeper flaw by pursuing the clue, the effort will
have been worth it. But if they get lost in obscure details that lead
nowhere, they'll have wasted their most precious resource: time.

To avoid chasing down the wrong clue, ask yourself the following questions:

- Is this path leading to something useful, or have I reached a dead end without realizing it?

- Is the potential outcome worth the time I'm spending?

- If I pause and reevaluate, will this still feel important?

- Am I staying focused on my goal? Is what I'm doing right now actually bringing me closer to achieving it?

It's easy to start with one goal and end up chasing a secondary objective that completely redirects your focus. Then the new objective quietly replaces the original goal without your even realizing it. Hackers avoid that by constantly reassessing whether their efforts are aligned with their primary objectives.

Being curious means exploring. Exploration can be filled with wonder *and* with traps. Dig deep when there's a good reason to do so, but if it feels like you're getting further from your goal rather than closer to it, pause and redirect your efforts. Learn the difference between a path that is worth investing effort in and one that is not. Your time and mental energy are limited resources—use them wisely.

QUICK RECAP

▶ Deeper understanding is the first step to finding new pathways.

▶ Asking why delivers insights that reveal flawed assumptions and overlooked shortcuts or loopholes.

▶ Implement the following tactics: go deeper with "The 5 Whys," determine the purpose of the system, analyze a different viewpoint, look at past performance, deliver your questions with care, and know when to stop digging.

For templates, exercises, and other tools to help you apply this, visit https://tedharrington.com/more.

Now that we've explored the power of asking why, let's use it to figure out how things work.

Hang On...Is This Even Okay?!

Before we go any further, let's pause for a gut check.

This book will teach you how to find (and then capitalize on) shortcuts and loopholes. Let's quickly examine what those are and why they are *good* (not bad). Then we'll address some concerns that this concept may raise for you.

A *shortcut* is an efficiency gain. It is a more direct way of achieving a goal—a way of bypassing steps in a process. A *loophole* is a gap or ambiguity. It provides an unintended way to bypass constraints and often stems from a flaw in a system.

Neither is bad. In fact, both are good. Most of us want to optimize our lives—to make things run more smoothly, eliminate unnecessary effort, and avoid wasting time. That's exactly what shortcuts do for you. They make things more efficient, and they make things better. Loopholes do, too. Things don't need to be *harder*; they need to be *easier*.

While writing this book, I struggled with the way those words might be interpreted. I remember once visiting a gym that I'd never been to before. There was a huge inspirational sign on the wall that said "There is no shortcut to sweat." That gave me pause. *Wait a minute*, I thought. *Are shortcuts cheating?*

No, shortcuts are not cheating. It is true that you cannot skip steps if you want to get fit,[5] but you absolutely *can* skip steps in, say,

---

5   Sure, things like steroids, weight-loss drugs, and even surgery can seem like shortcuts to fitness. But they don't build real health—just the illusion of it. Worse, they often come at a tremendous cost: organ damage, hormonal imbalances, mental health issues, or long-term dependence. Not exactly a "shortcut" to any outcome a health-conscious person might be aiming for.

a bureaucratic process and still get the results you desire. In fact, it would be unwise not to do that if it's possible.

You may be wondering why you should capitalize on shortcuts and loopholes, so let me put it plainly: because they exist, because other people are using them, and because you'll get left behind if you don't. Furthermore, they are the result of inefficiencies, bloat, and flawed choices. Why let those things guide your life? Shortcuts and loopholes are there to *help* you.

Consider the classic board game Chutes and Ladders. The goal is to advance your game piece to the end of a long twisting pathway. The first person there wins. Within the game, there are "ladders" that help you advance up the pathway faster by avoiding some of the twists and turns. That's exactly what we are talking about here: simply taking a better path. The ladders are part of the game. They are there for you to use. Whether you do or do not, others will.

Moreover, even if you use the shortcuts and loopholes available to you, your challenge will still be difficult. It will require perseverance, time, and optimism. You can't skip the hard work required to reach a goal. However, you can simplify that work by removing some of the unnecessary twists and turns. And that's what hackers do. They're always looking for the chutes and ladders that will make a process better or worse.

Remember: Hackers aren't inherently good or bad. Hackers are just *hackers*: curious, non-conforming, committed, creative problem solvers. What separates the good from the bad is what drives them. Malicious hackers seek to gain something for themselves—like notoriety, profit, or power—and they're fine hurting others to get it. Ethical hackers may also want recognition or success, but they're guided by a different compass: They want to make things *better*. They're *not* okay with causing harm. You're here to think like a hacker, but be the kind that helps, not hurts.

In biology, there is a concept called *symbiosis*, which refers to a close and long-term interaction between two different species. There are a few types of symbiotic relationships, including one called *mutualism*, which is beneficial to both species. For example, take the relationship between a bee and a flower: The bee gets food while the flower gets pollinated. When you apply the hacker mindset to your life, that's the kind of relationship you'll want to engage in: one in which you help yourself *while* helping others.

In parasitic relationships, on the other hand, one party benefits at the expense of the other. For example, a mosquito feasts on human blood, leaving its victim with itchy, irritated skin—and sometimes even spreading deadly diseases in the process.

Be the bee, not the mosquito.

Use the hacker mindset for good, not for harm.

Be like this → 🐝 🦟 ← Not like this

With that said, let's examine some common concerns people have when they are first introduced to the hacker mindset—especially when applying it outside the world of computers. Is it ethical? Legal? Fair? Let's look at each.

Is this ethical?

Yes, when you act with integrity—that is, with honesty, consistency, and respect for others. If you don't, it's not ethical.

There is a general code of conduct you can follow to apply the hacker mindset without breaking any ethical boundaries. It's pretty simple.

1. **Do not violate others:** Don't rob, cheat, or exploit anyone.

2. **Create value:** Make things better for yourself and those around you.

Follow that code, and you'll be good to apply the principles in this book.

Is this legal?

Yes, you can apply the hacker mindset to almost anything—as long as you don't break the law.

I know that seems like a cheeky answer, but it really is that simple.[6]

Is this fair?

Unfortunately, life isn't fair.

If it were, you'd already have the things you deserve. Everyone would. You wouldn't need a book to teach you new ways to achieve your goals, navigate change, and level up.

Everything you want to do exists in the context of a larger system. That system is governed by rules. Those rules are (probably) not designed to treat everyone fairly.

Don't shoot the messenger. That's just the game.

Consider the US tax code. It is designed to encourage

---

6 Later in this book, I'll show you why you can (and should) break the law in select cases. However, those cases are rare exceptions, so for now, let's just keep it at "don't break the law."

entrepreneurship. As a result, the people who get the best tax breaks are business owners, while the people who get the worst tax breaks are employees.

Is it fair? That's not really for me to say.

Is it the game? *Yes.*

The question isn't really about fairness but about whether you want to play the game.

I won't make many absolute statements in this book, but I will make three here:

1. Loopholes and shortcuts exist.

2. Other people are already capitalizing on them.

3. If you do so within ethical boundaries, capitalizing on them is good (and it's definitely not bad).

So it's up to you.

Is using the hacker mindset fair? Maybe yes, maybe no.

Is the *game* fair? Definitely no.

Should you exploit the advantages available to you? Definitely yes.

You're chasing something hard to achieve. You'll need every advantage you can get to achieve it. You now have a book full of ideas that will help you capture those advantages.

Go get them.

CHAPTER 2

FIGURE OUT HOW IT WORKS

When you learn how things are supposed to work, you learn how they might fail, too.

Can you start a fire from the internet?

It might sound like a wild thought, but that's the essence of hacking: asking questions no one else is asking.

One of our hackers at ISE became curious about that question. As part of a cool piece of security research he did before joining the company, Joel looked into an internet-connected power strip. He theorized that if he could hack the power strip and use it to manipulate the power supplied to the devices plugged into it, he might be able to cause one to catch fire.

Over several weeks, Joel methodically explored how the power strip worked. Step by step, he dissected the functionality of the hardware, firmware, and associated web application (a web management portal). That helped him figure out how to attack it. Eventually, he identified vulnerabilities that when exploited in sequence, enabled him to remotely cycle the power strip on and off. And then he figured out how to remotely control *other users'* power strips too.[7]

Then he needed to test his theory by abusing the devices plugged into the power strip. So he bought a bunch of antique appliances, such as old lamps that predated modern fire safety standards. He wrote code to make the power strip rapidly cycle on and off. Then he plugged those sketchy old lamps into the power strip, hoping to see one of them catch fire. That caused a loud terrifying sound. Joel's wife hated it. However, it didn't result in a fire. The power strip's hardware relay burned out first, cutting his experiment short.

When Joel shared that story with me, I couldn't help but ask, "Why share a story where the main goal wasn't achieved?"

His answer was simple and powerful: "Even though it didn't lead to a fire, it *did* result in a breach of the network. That alone was an important finding. But more importantly, it was one of the most complex vulnerability chains I've ever written."

Then Joel said something that made me grin from ear to ear:

---

7   If you're interested in the technical details, here's how his exploit worked: An attacker (in this case, Joel) crafts a website designed to deliver a malicious payload and induces a user of the power strip's web management portal to visit it. That user is then hit with a "drive-by" attack in which the payload (embedded in a cookie) is delivered to the user and stored in their browser. Later, when the victim visits the portal, the payload is executed, altering the login form and capturing the user's credentials. The payload then exploits a command injection vulnerability in the authenticated portion of the portal, giving the attacker system-level access. In that way, the attacker gains raw control over the outlet states (on and off).

"The thing about hackers is that if they don't know how something works, they're compelled to figure it out."

Joel detailed how each roadblock in the project had taught him something new, preparing him for future challenges. That power strip experiment, though unsuccessful in its immediate goal, directly influenced his work on a consulting project later. Joel recently performed a security assessment for a client of ours that had developed a widely used video streaming app. He identified a critical vulnerability that could have caused *catastrophic* financial losses for our client if it had been exploited by an attacker. Thanks to the skills he'd honed during the power strip project, as well as other research he'd done over the years, he was able to develop a proof-of-concept exploit in just a few hours. (Remember, that is a good thing! The whole point of ethical hacking is for the good guys to find and fix the flaws before the bad guys find and exploit them.)

When I asked Joel what motivates him to figure out how systems work, his answer was beautiful: "Simple—it's so I can hack things. Finding a good vulnerability is almost like a drug. It makes me feel good for a week or more. It gives me a sense of accomplishment. It keeps me happy." He continued. "One of the reasons I keep doing this is to encounter vulnerabilities I've never seen before and to find novel ways to exploit them. I learn something new with every project."

Hackers are relentlessly curious. They want to understand how things work because it's often the only way to find those hidden flaws. That relentless need to figure out how things work is what makes them so effective at what they do. Before they can hack something, they must understand its mechanics, its rules, and its limits. That curiosity is the starting point for everything they go on to achieve.

Joel's story also highlights a crucial lesson: Mastery isn't about instant success. It's about failing, learning, and trying again. Every experiment, every failure, and every discovery builds the skills and knowledge needed to achieve something bigger. For Joel, the power strip project wasn't about starting a fire—it was about learning how the system worked, which prepared him to solve much bigger problems later.

Hackers excel because they constantly push themselves to learn, improve, and adapt. They aren't afraid to fail, and they view every challenge as an opportunity to grow. That mindset is what makes them exceptional.

The same principle applies to any change or goal in life. Whatever you're pursuing, start by figuring out how it works. Be curious. Ask questions. Dig deep into the mechanics of the problem you're solving. Once you understand the system, you can find new and creative ways to achieve your goals.

Relentless curiosity makes hackers special.

It works for them. It will work for you too.

Observing This Mindset in the Real World

Many years ago, before leaping into the hacking world with Steve, I didn't know much about cybersecurity. (I often still feel that way, to be honest. There's always so much more to learn.) That was a problem, and a pretty big one at that:

I was about to run a security company and didn't know the first damn thing about security.

Funny how life can sneak up on you like that.

So I did what hackers do: I figured out how it worked.

I became insatiably curious about security concepts. What causes a system to be hacked? How do we prevent that? What skills do our people need in order to be elite? I wanted to learn everything I possibly could. I became a sponge for information.

I turned to our security analysts, asking them endless questions. I can't even count how many times I said some version of "Okay, but explain that to me like I'm five years old." I talked to friends, colleagues, people I met at conferences, and even strangers online. As people fielded my questions, their answers invariably included some terms, concepts, or details that I wasn't familiar with. I wanted to learn about those, too. I had no ego about it—being a novice is exhilarating. I was excited to keep asking questions, no matter how basic they were.

Eventually, things started to click. I slowly started to understand the concepts. I learned the terms. I figured out why things work the way they do (and why they might work differently if conditions changed). It took years, but eventually, I figured it out. I learned by reading, asking questions, keeping an open mind, not letting my pride get in the way, and fully embracing my status as a novice.

Fast-forward to today, and I'm able to write books like this one.

The point is this: Although I know about security *now*, that certainly was not always the case. But as a hacker once told me, "Being inquisitive is more important than having technical skills." Eventually, through relentless curiosity, I was able to figure it out. Let's talk about how you can do that too.

How to Apply This to Your Life

Hackers are masters at gathering information, and if you apply a few of their techniques, you can be, too.

TACTIC #1 Gather OSINT.

Open-source intelligence (OSINT) gathering refers to the collection and analysis of open-source data with the goal of producing action-able intelligence. Basically, it is the act of learning about a system by

```
                    ┌─────────┐
                    │ Gather  │
                    │  OSINT  │
                    └─────────┘
┌──────────┐                      ┌──────────────┐
│   Be     │                      │     Ask      │
│ skeptical│                      │  open-ended  │
│          │                      │  questions   │
└──────────┘                      └──────────────┘

        [ FIGURE OUT HOW IT WORKS ]

┌────────────────┐                ┌──────────┐
│Reverse-engineer│                │ Explore  │
│  the outcome   │                │cause and │
│                │                │  effect  │
└────────────────┘                └──────────┘
                    ┌─────────┐
                    │Develop a│
                    │system map│
                    └─────────┘
```

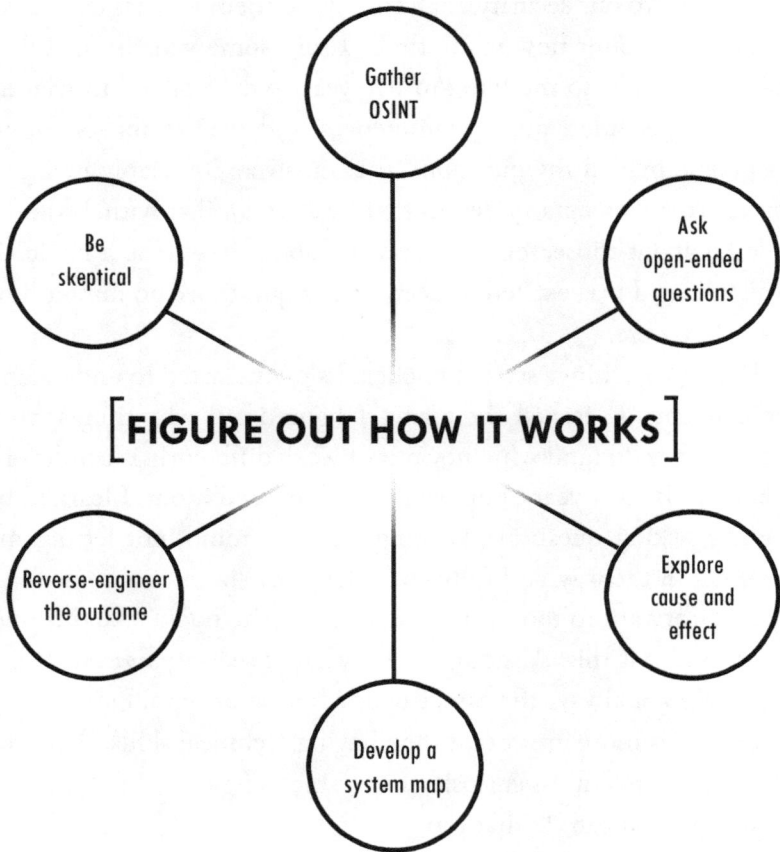

studying publicly available information about it. It helps you build out a mental map of the landscape you're investigating so that you can start envisioning ways you might abuse or attack it.

Gathering OSINT is like playing the board game Clue. The objective is to figure out who committed a murder, in what room, with what weapon. The gameplay involves asking a series of questions to eliminate suspects, locations, and murder weapons. Through deductive reasoning, you solve the mystery. OSINT gathering is similar: You collect publicly available information from which you deduce insights that will help you pursue your goal.

Unlike malicious hackers, who can devote as much time as they'd like to their "projects," ethical hackers have limited time for exploration. Working under time and budget constraints, ethical hackers must gather as much information as possible before launching an attack sequence to maximize efficiency and improve their chance of success.

Hackers read support documentation, white papers, and marketing collateral when gathering OSINT. They watch talks delivered by executives, and they research developers on social media. They sign up for demos and sit through sales pitches.

As you think about your goal, gather all the publicly available information you can. A few simple searches—online or at a library—can uncover crucial details: who's involved, how the process works, what matters, and how decisions get made. Like in the game of Clue, these facts will help you piece things together later.

TACTIC #2 Ask open-ended questions.

When scoping out a security assessment, hackers often ask the client open-ended questions.[8] Open-ended questions are those that cannot be answered with a simple yes or no and are meant to elicit a deeper, more thorough answer. Asking open-ended questions during scoping spurs the client to provide context and details—including details on things that the hackers don't even know to ask about. It is important to avoid boxing the client in and pushing the discussion

---

8 *Scoping* is consultant-speak for the process of defining what a project will and won't include. *Testing* is when we get into hands-on exploration of the system and actively look for security vulnerabilities.

down a finite path. Instead, the client should be allowed to drive the discussion wherever it needs to go.

For example, a hacker might ask an open-ended question such as "Can you please describe the application's authorization functionality?" rather than a closed-ended question such as "Does the application use role-based access controls?" The former allows for a much richer and more nuanced answer, while the latter leaves room only for a yes or no, neither of which would be very helpful on its own.

As you think about your goal, work to ask open-ended questions. Just as hackers talk to the client before starting an assessment, you'll want to talk to people directly involved in or knowledgeable about your goal to make sure you understand what to do. Talk to people who have done it before, people who make approvals, people who influence decisions, or vendors you may need to hire. Explore the way things usually work.

Be sure to ask *loads* of open-ended questions. The more questions you ask, the more information you'll gather. Eventually, you'll stumble upon something that no one else thought was important and find it is the key that unlocks everything.

TACTIC #3 Explore cause and effect.

"What would happen if an attacker did X?"

We usually ask some version of that question during the scoping phase of an assessment (and hackers definitely ask themselves some version of it during the testing phase). It's as much a thought exercise as it is a way to guide deeper investigation. The purpose of the question is to uncover two things: (1) what would happen as a result of a given action and (2) why *that* action would cause *that* result. Importantly, you'll want to examine the assumptions that are built into that cause-and-effect relationship. (We'll explore assumptions later in the book.)

As you explore the ways that people typically achieve the goal you're pursuing, think about the actions you could take, the outcomes those actions tend to produce, and the reasons for those outcomes. You can approach that process systematically in three steps.

First, identify the variables, or the parts of the process that can be modified and may influence the outcome. Examples include the resources you use, your timing, your strategy, and the environment.

Second, experiment with the variables. Test each one individually by changing it; then observe the change's impact on the results.

Third, analyze the outcomes. Trace the results of specific actions back to their causes to understand why those outcomes were produced. Study the impact of each change to your variables to uncover insights and optimize your approach.

In the previous chapter, you read about the power of asking why. This tactic is one of the many places you'll want to apply the concepts you've learned. By seeking a deeper understanding of the relationship between actions and their outcomes, you'll learn more about the goal you're chasing (and about yourself too).

TACTIC #4 Develop a system map.

System mapping is a process by which you identify key information about a system. (Remember, everything exists within the context of a system, including the goal you are chasing.) Basically, you diagram the different components of the system and those components' interactions with one another. Through system mapping, hackers determine the overall architecture of a system, which helps them understand where they should focus their efforts, time, and resources. When you know how a thing is built, you can figure out how to attack it.

Hackers create system maps through a number of steps, such as running port scans, performing Domain Name System interrogation, and enumerating Lightweight Directory Access Protocol services.[9] What those terms mean isn't important. What *is* important is that there are discrete steps that can be taken to gather concrete information about a target system. Those steps can be taken in a systematic, scalable, and repeatable way.

The same is true of the system in which your goal exists. You'll want to identify the people, processes, and decision-making forums that are relevant to your goal. Go write it all down. If possible, create a system map. It doesn't need to be fancy; it can be as simple as a whiteboard diagram with lines connecting the various components.

Once you have all of the information, you can begin to understand how it all works together. That understanding will be crucial when you implement the techniques discussed later in this book.

TACTIC #5 Reverse-engineer the outcome.

To reverse-engineer is to systematically analyze a system or product to understand how it works, often without any prior knowledge of its design or construction. The process usually focuses on reconstructing the logic, design, or functionality of a system. For example, an ethical hacker might take a proprietary software system and disassemble its code to see how it handles user authentication. In doing so, the hacker might discover a flaw in the authentication process that allows for unauthorized access.

You can reverse-engineer almost anything in life, including (and especially) the process of navigating a moment of change, achieving a goal, or leveling up your life. Here are a few simple steps you can take to do that.

---

9   I use these terms only to provide examples of actions that hackers take to gather information. The steps you'll take to gather information about your goal will have their own unique vocabulary.

First, start with the outcome. Define a clear goal. Articulate what you want to achieve, and be specific. A clear destination will help you reverse-engineer the path you need to take. For example, you might state, "I want to run a successful online business that generates $100,000 in annual revenue."

Second, study the typical path. Analyze how others have achieved your goal. Break down the steps, identify common patterns, and seek to understand what worked for them. If no comparable models exist, try to define a path anyway, identifying the things you believe will be necessary for you to achieve the desired outcome. Those elements are the components of success.

Take our example of building an online business that generates $100,000 in annual revenue. Studying the typical path might mean researching successful e-commerce entrepreneurs to understand the skills they developed, the tools they used, and the milestones they hit on the way to success.

Third, map out the process. Work backward, step by step, to build your plan. Start from the end and identify the necessary steps in reverse order. Focus on the dependencies—the things that need to happen before each step—and prioritize accordingly. Working backward will ensure that you don't miss any steps and that your plan is rooted in practical milestones rather than vague aspirations.

Let's return to our online business example. A map of the steps might look something like this:

1. **Final outcome:** Bring in $100,000 in annual revenue.

2. **Step before that:** Build a go-to-market strategy that includes sales and marketing channels.

3. **Step before that:** Create a compelling product or service that solves a pain point.

4. **Step before that:** Identify customer pain points.

5. **Step before that:** Identify an audience to serve.

TACTIC #6 Be skeptical.

Hackers refuse to take things at face value. They prefer to do their own investigation instead of just accepting what they're told. Hackers know that the flaws in a system are usually the result of human error—especially errors in assumptions. When someone tells a hacker that something *cannot be done*, the hacker usually responds with "Challenge accepted!"

Resist the temptation to believe something is true just because it's generally *held* to be true. Being skeptical is a good way to stimulate curiosity and a good way to figure out how things work. It leads you to probe for information, pull on threads, ask follow-up questions, and dig deeper. As you pursue your goals, remain skeptical. Be wary of what is generally accepted to be true.

Here is a simple exercise that you can perform to remain skeptical in the pursuit of curiosity. Whenever you hear someone state something as a fact, run through three questions:

1. Why does this person think that?

2. Could the opposite be true?

3. Is there a different way?

There's a saying that is central to the security profession: Trust but verify. It essentially means that we can move forward on important tasks, but in the process, we should double-check what we're being told. Skepticism leads to truth; apply that idea in your pursuit of your goal and see what unfolds.

QUICK RECAP

▶ When you learn how things are supposed to work, you learn how they might fail, too.

▶ Before you can find the loopholes and shortcuts in a system, you need to understand how the system works.

▶ Implement the following tactics: gather OSINT, ask open-ended questions, explore cause and effect, develop a system map, reverse-engineer the outcome, and be skeptical.

For templates, exercises, and other tools to help you apply this, visit https://tedharrington.com/more.

Now that you've taken it apart, looked at it from the inside, and figured out how it works, let's recap part I, "Hackers Are Curious." Then we'll move on to part II, "Hackers Are Non-Conforming."

Hackers Are
CURIOUS

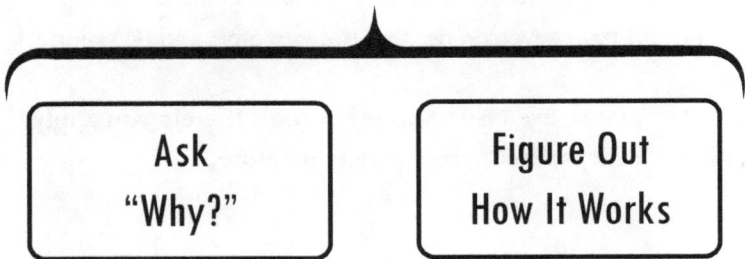

Ask "Why?"	Figure Out How It Works

Curiosity enables hackers to find new and unexpected pathways to achieving their goals. Here's how you can be relentlessly curious too:

Ask "Why?"

- *Go deeper with "The 5 Whys"* so that you can get past the surface level and understand things in a deeper and more meaningful way.

- *Determine the purpose of the system* to figure out where to look for flawed assumptions or poorly implemented functionality.

- *Analyze a different viewpoint* to understand how someone else might think about a situation and potentially uncover overlooked opportunities.

- *Look at past performance* to learn what worked (or didn't work), and let those lessons inform your next step.

- *Deliver your questions with care*, because asking why is sometimes interpreted as a judgment, an attack, or a signal of distrust—and a misinterpretation like that won't help you reach your goal.

- *Know when to stop digging* to avoid going down trails that won't get you closer to your goal.

Figure Out How It Works

- *Gather OSINT* and use the information you learn to craft a strategy for reaching your goal.

- *Ask open-ended questions* to elicit nuanced, contextual answers that will lead you to helpful insights.

- *Explore cause and effect* to better understand why certain actions cause certain results and identify ways to adjust your approach.

- *Develop a system map* to collect and organize key information that will help you reach your goal.

- *Reverse-engineer the outcome* to determine the steps you'll need to take.

- *Be skeptical* as a way to find the truth.

PART II

HACKERS ARE NON-CONFORMING

CHAPTER 3

CHALLENGE ASSUMPTIONS

Conformist thinking means trusting assumptions without questioning them. Challenging those assumptions reveals the flaws they contain.

Can dating be hacked?

If you've been in the dating pool any time since 2012 or so, you've probably used a dating app in your search for love. Have you ever wondered whether the information that users give those apps is actually secure?

The team at ISE sure has.

Sanjana, one of our hackers, became interested in the topic and set out to research the security vulnerabilities that might exist in dating apps. She focused on a few of the major apps, such as Bumble and Hinge.

(Brace yourself: If you already think modern dating is a mess, this story is not going to make you feel any better.)

After a few months, she had found some shocking results:

1. *Attackers could change vote data.* A "vote" is a user's decision about whether they are interested or uninterested in a potential match (usually expressed through swiping right or swiping left). That hottie rejected you? Not anymore! Just change the hottie's vote so that you'll be matched!

2. *Attackers could get the premium version for free.* Most apps operate on a "freemium" model: You can get basic functionality for free, or you can upgrade your account to get access to the features you need. Want those premium features without paying for them? Just bypass the payment controls!

3. *Attackers could triangulate users' locations.* Perhaps the most terrifying finding was that user location data is easy to discover. Did that hottie ghost you? Just go to their house!

So what caused these security issues?[10]

As is often the case, they were the result of flawed assumptions made by the companies that developed the applications. We discov-

---

10 I'll explain the story at a high level; if you'd like to read the technical details of this groundbreaking research, you can find them at https://tedharrington. com/more.

ered many flawed assumptions, but let me highlight just one, which first requires us to talk about brute-force attacks.

In a brute-force attack, a malicious actor attempts to identify a user's credentials, the value of an encryption key, or another value by systematically trying all possible combinations of characters. There is a well-understood, easy-to-implement, highly effective technique for preventing brute-force attacks called *rate limiting*.

You've likely encountered rate limiting without realizing it. Consider this common scenario: You try to log in to a website or application and accidentally enter the wrong password. You then try another password, and that one is wrong too. After a few more failed login attempts, you're locked out of your account. That's rate limiting. Rate limiting helps prevent brute forcing and other kinds of attacks by limiting the number of requests (e.g., login attempts) that a user can make within a certain period.

Well, despite the effectiveness of the technique, several of the dating apps that Sanjana investigated lacked rate limiting. The omission revealed an important flawed assumption: the assumption that no one would attempt a brute-force attack. Unfortunately, there are malicious people out there who *absolutely* would (and probably have). Pretty much everything gets attacked pretty much every single day. Whether that assumption was *intentional* (i.e., the companies actively decided that no one would attempt an attack) or *unintentional* (i.e., they didn't even think about it), the result was the same: Their systems were vulnerable to brute-force attacks.

Flawed assumptions are the soft underbelly of every weak system. Humans make assumptions about all kinds of things: what other people will or won't do, what something will require, and how long something will take, for example. By identifying and challenging those assumptions, hackers find exploitable security vulnerabilities.

This concept is a central component of non-conformist thinking. When other people accept what they're told, follow assumptions without question, and go about their lives without independent thought, you'll want to do the opposite. By refusing to conform, you'll find the loopholes, shortcuts, and overlooked opportunities that everyone else has missed.

Observing This Mindset in the Real World

If you live in Southern California, you need a car.

Or do you?

If you have ever visited Los Angeles, San Diego, or the beautiful coastal towns in between, you've probably noticed that everything is spread out and that the public transportation system is weak. Perhaps you've also noticed something more significant but maybe not as obvious: The people there simply like cars. To a resident of Southern California, having a vehicle signifies freedom, autonomy, and (unfortunately) status.

I first moved to San Diego in 2006, and (as is often the case for San Diego transplants) one of the first things I did was buy a car. It was a bright-red Pontiac Sunfire convertible, and I loved it. A convertible is an absurd choice for someone like me who gets sunburned almost immediately after stepping outside. But I found the most profound joy in hopping into the car with the top already down and then enjoying the sea breeze as I drove around town. I hated the traffic, but I sure loved the driving experience.

Several years later, I moved to Baltimore, where Steve and I chose to headquarter our security companies. I sold my beloved convertible and, when I got to Maryland, bought a car more suitable for a consistently terrible climate. (I mean *terrible*. It's always too hot, too cold, or too rainy. Not exactly convertible weather.)

I chose a sporty Volkswagen CC Coupe with a six-speed manual transmission. Limited-edition gold paint, hand-stitched leather interior, all of the upgrades. I loved it.

However, I didn't really drive it much. I lived only a couple of miles from the office; after a full year, I realized that I'd put fewer than 3,000 miles on it.

That was when I first started wondering, *Do I need a car?*

The thought surprised me. I loved my car.

I quickly dismissed the idea. I lived close to the office, but not quite close enough. Too inconvenient for transit, too exposed to inclement weather to walk, too uphill to bike. *Like it or not*, I thought, *I do need a car.*

Then, a year and a half later, it became time to open a West Coast office. Back to California I went.

That time, however, it was different.

Instead of immediately going to the dealership, I paused to think about car ownership. I had always assumed that I *needed* a car. I had always assumed that it was one of life's necessities, like housing and groceries.

But...was it?

Did I really need a car?

I'd been operating under an assumption that I had not yet examined. So I decided to start asking questions.

Did I need a car to commute? Only if it would be inconvenient to use other methods.

Did I like driving? If I was being honest, not really. I would have fun taking short drives on wide open roads—but I also hated a lot of what driving actually entails. I loathed the irrational, unpredictable, dangerous choices that other drivers made. I hated sitting in traffic, looking for parking, being tired and bored, worrying about mechanical failures, dealing with repairs, and worrying about damage or theft.

I started asking myself whether there might be a better way.

When I first lived in California in 2006, ridesharing hadn't been invented yet. By the time I returned in 2014, companies like Uber had established ridesharing as a viable option. I started to explore whether I could use it full time rather than owning a car.

What I discovered really surprised me: It's actually less expensive to use ridesharing full time than it is to own a car.

If you're like *almost everyone* I've ever said that to, you probably don't believe me.

So let me show you the numbers.

	Financial comparison	
	Car ownership ($)	Full-time ridesharing ($)
Car payment	500	0
Insurance	100	0
Parking	50–250	0
Maintenance	100–200	0
Registration	50	0
Ridesharing	50–200	400–550
TOTAL	850–1,300	400–550

Table 1. A breakdown of the monthly costs of car ownership and ridesharing use. Onetime or annual expenses have been divided across the 12 months to facilitate comparison.

The figures in table 1 assume a midrange car like a base model Jeep Cherokee, and they would skyrocket if we considered a higher-performance, luxury, or status-symbol car instead.[11] As you can see, the costs creep up fast.

––––––––––––

11 These are the actual expenses I incurred as a car owner between 2011 and 2014 in Maryland and California. Costs today are almost certainly much higher across the board, so a comparison between present-day car ownership and ridesharing would be even more extreme.

Keep in mind that even if you own a car, you'll probably still spend at least *some* money on ridesharing. Maybe you'll need rides to the airport or to events involving alcohol, or maybe you'll end up traveling in other cities without your car.

Considered on its own, spending $500 or more per month on ridesharing might sound *ludicrous*. But when you compare that amount to the total cost of car ownership, the decision looks pretty savvy.

The difference becomes even more exciting when you evaluate what I consider to be far more important than cost savings: the mental health benefits.

	Mental health comparison	
	Car ownership	Full-time ridesharing
Driving in traffic	Stress	No stress
Finding parking	Stress	No stress
Worrying about maintenance	Stress	No stress
Worrying about theft/damage	Stress	No stress

Table 2. The effects of car ownership and full-time ridesharing on mental health

Once I'd written it all out, it seemed *absolutely bonkers* to me that I'd once thought that I "needed" a car. What an absurd assumption I'd never paused to question.

Once I recognized and then challenged that assumption, I realized that owning a car was holding me back, both financially and mentally.

I never did buy a car after returning to California. For more than eleven years (and counting!), I've maintained a completely car-free lifestyle despite living in one of the most car-dependent regions in America. I am saving money while simultaneously—and much more importantly—eliminating a lot of stress. I challenged a long-held assumption, and as a result, my life instantly improved.[12]

When you challenge assumptions, you find better ways to live and work.

There's a reason that chain restaurants like the Cheesecake Factory are successful but don't win coveted culinary awards like Michelin stars: They appeal to the masses, and excellence doesn't exist among the masses. Those who live in the herd are, by definition, not exceptional.

You're reading a book that will help you think differently, so I'd guess that at least part of you identifies as exceptional. So why would you want to blend in? Why would you want to conform with the masses?

Achieving excellence requires you to stand out. You need to be different. You need to blaze new trails.

That might be scary, but trust me—it is the way.

How to Apply This to Your Life

There are two steps involved in making this mindset shift: First you need to identify your assumptions, and then you need to challenge them. The former is a lot harder than it sounds, so we'll explore a few ways to do that first and then dive into ways to challenge those assumptions.

---

12 I remain open to changing my mind on this someday if my circumstances change. Someday, it might make more sense to own a car than to be car-free. If that happens, I'll approach the situation with the same sense of non-conformity. I'll assess the circumstances and determine the best path. I'll let go of any attachment to prior decisions I've made or perceptions that others may have. I will decide for myself. I will not be guided by what others or society or conventional thinking would suggest I must do. That's what it means to challenge assumptions. You think freely and independently. You find the best way *for you*.

TACTIC #1 **Ask other people.**

Hackers are very collaborative people. I commonly observe them asking one another questions like "Am I looking at this right?" and "What am I missing?" and "Any idea how to get past this?" Hackers are adept at seeking other viewpoints.

That is important because it's pretty hard to see your own assumptions. After all, assumptions are things that you accept to be true—often without realizing. Assumptions tend to be invisible, hiding in plain sight. A good way to solve this problem is to ask friends, family, or trusted advisors to help you. Ask them what *they* think *you* assume to be true about a given situation.

That might be tricky at first, because it's an unusual thing to ask people—but hey, hackers are unusual people. Be patient while the person helping you figures out what you're getting at, and listen closely to their response.

Other people can observe things about you that you have difficulty seeing yourself. For example, one of my childhood friends is a super smart guy whom I admire deeply. I've known him literally my whole life. When he applied to business school years ago, he asked for my help with his essay. We often say that we've known each other since the womb, and he was very curious to learn about my perception of him and whether I'd observed something that he might not have seen in himself. However, since I'd never seen him in a business setting, I didn't know much about his leadership style. So I did what any curious person would do: I asked lots of questions.

At that point, he hadn't really considered that there were different leadership styles at all. He'd thought leadership was just leadership. Of course, that assumption is flawed, so it turned out to be a great place for us to dig deeper. I asked about his philosophies, what he was most proud of, what he wanted to improve, how he preferred to lead, and how he liked to be led. More importantly, *he* asked *me* lots of questions about my views of him. I asked questions about who he admired as a leader and why; he asked me loads of questions about my views on his strengths, weaknesses, and style.

Eventually, he figured out which leadership style he most identified with: servant leadership. Through our question-and-answer exercise, it became clear that the servant leadership mindset was something he already possessed on the inside *and* the part of himself that he wanted to cultivate. With that clarity, he made the concept of servant leadership central to his application essay.

As you might imagine, he was accepted to his top-choice program. Fast-forward to today, and he's a senior executive at one of the biggest consumer product companies in the world. He loves his job. As far as I can tell, he has become exactly the kind of leader he hoped to grow into.

If you want to challenge your assumptions, you need to know what they are—but you probably can't see them on your own. Your friends, family, and colleagues see you from a different viewpoint and aren't as shackled by your assumptions.[13] Enlist the help of others, and you'll have an easier time identifying your own assumptions. Then you'll be able to challenge them.

TACTIC #2 Listen to understand.

Hackers are skilled at gathering information. They pick up on details and nuance. Hackers ask questions (and clarifying questions about their answers) and generally seek to understand.

However, most people aren't like that. How often have you told a story about something that happened and barely finished before someone else jumped in with "Something like that happened to me" and then told their own story right on top of yours? That's a sign of someone who is listening to *respond*, not listening to *understand*. Try not to be like that, please. I suggest that partly because it's annoying, but mostly because it runs counter to the hacker mindset.

There's nothing wrong with positively contributing to a conversation by sharing stories, ideas, and viewpoints (in fact, you should do that—it's the point of conversation). However, most people don't listen intently to others. They wait for others to shut up so they can

---

13 Keep in mind, however, that they will have their own assumptions too, and they'll be just as oblivious to them as you are to yours.

steer the conversation back to their favorite topic: themselves.

That is listening to *respond*, when instead you want to listen to *understand*.

When you're listening to *respond* rather than listening to *understand*, you completely miss the cues, insights, and opportunities that could lead to deeper understanding. That means you miss the opportunities to identify assumptions that could otherwise be challenged—whether they are assumptions you hold or assumptions held by the person to whom you're listening.

The antidote is practicing active listening and asking clarifying questions. Every single time you hear a new perspective on an idea, compare it to your existing view on the topic. Consider whether that perspective is a valid way of thinking. Is it different from what you already think? Is it better, worse, or similar? What new ideas does it inspire?

Steve is one of the most brilliant people I've ever met. He knows so much about so much that it's almost breathtaking. Nevertheless, he's always listening with the intent of challenging his own assumptions. Even when he has a firmly cemented view on something, he is curious about whether he should change his mind.

When I was thinking about writing this book, Steve wasn't really on board at first. *Hackable* was already out in the market, it was crushing it in terms of sales (#1 bestseller, baby!), and it had already done great things for our businesses, both directly and indirectly. Why did we need another book? he asked. Wouldn't my efforts be better spent on something else? He was pretty resolute in his stance that I shouldn't spend my finite amount of time writing another book. But he heard me out anyway. Once he understood why this book mattered and who it would help and how, he changed his mind.

I didn't need Steve's blessing to write this book, but he's my business partner and one of my closest friends; I wanted us to be aligned, especially on something as big, challenging, and meaningful as writing a book. Steve is the very definition of a hacker, so although he entered the discussion with a pretty firm idea about how we should proceed, he kept his mind open, and he listened to understand. That guided his thinking.

Even when you are *absolutely certain* about something, make sure to listen to understand. You may surprise yourself by finding that some of the assumptions behind your certainty are actually flawed.

TACTIC #3 Test absolutes.

Hackers are scientists, and scientists generally don't use absolute terms such as *always* or *never*. There are usually exceptions to absolute statements, and where there are exceptions, you'll likely find overlooked assumptions or flaws that you can use to your advantage.

People, especially system designers, use absolute statements all the time. Hackers tend to look for areas that are indicative of absolute thinking, as they're good areas to probe for weaknesses. For example, consider the absolute term *must*. Systems are often set up such that

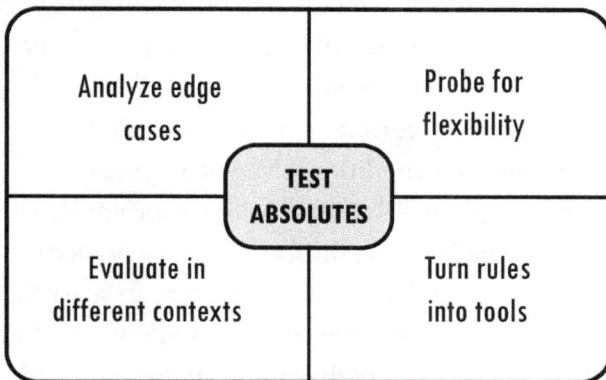

they "must" do *X*. A hacker would ask, What would happen if it didn't do *X*? What if I found a way to bypass that requirement? Exploring questions like those often leads them to flaws in the system.

That idea applies to both technical systems and life. Whenever you hear absolute statements, test them. Common examples of absolute terms include *always, never, all, none, every, must, must not, cannot, forever, completely,* and—perhaps above all—*impossible.* Whenever you hear one of those terms, recognize that you've found an area worth exploring. You might find flawed assumptions that will lead to helpful shortcuts, loopholes, and new pathways.

Here are four ways to test absolutes.

First, analyze the edge cases. Edge cases are situations that arise under rare or extreme conditions. When you look more closely at the edge cases in a system, you automatically challenge the absolutes that the system claims to uphold. Consider NASA's preparations for space missions. The agency operates in an environment of absolutes: Astronauts *must* stay alive. Spacecraft systems *cannot* fail without a backup plan. To ensure success, NASA pushes every system and protocol to its absolute limits, testing extreme scenarios such as sudden atmospheric decompression and exposure to high-radiation zones. Even things as mundane as duct tape are subjected to testing under zero gravity and extreme temperatures. By identifying when and where a system could fail, NASA addresses potential vulnerabilities before astronauts encounter them.

In your life or work, consider where absolutes might fail under extreme or unexpected conditions. Maybe a system at your workplace assumes people will "always" follow a protocol. What happens when someone is in a rush? Or perhaps a marketing strategy assumes customers will "never" use a feature in a particular way, but what if they do? Testing the edge cases allows you to find new insights, opportunities, and pathways to success.

Second, probe for flexibility. Providing unexpected input to a rigid system often causes it to break; in fact, that's one of the ways hackers gain a foothold in a system. Consider Casper's approach to selling mattresses. Mattress companies traditionally relied on third-party showrooms and high-pressure sales tactics, assuming customers would always want to lie on a mattress before buying it. When it first launched, Casper tested that "absolute" by selling mattresses online and offering a generous return policy. It allowed customers to try mattresses at home and to return them if the customers didn't like them. By rethinking the typical distribution model, it bypassed traditional retail middlemen and built a direct relationship with customers, setting off a wave of mattress-in-a-box start-ups and disrupting a stagnant industry.[14]

Think about the absolutes in your own work that might be more flexible than they appear. Are there rigid processes, assumptions, or norms that everyone accepts and no one has challenged? Probe those areas, and you might uncover opportunities to bypass bottlenecks, streamline efforts, or create entirely new ways of working. Breaking away from traditional paths and testing for flexibility could enable you to identify a much better way just as it did for Casper.

Third, evaluate absolutes in different contexts. Test whether an absolute holds up across various environments. If a claim falls apart in some situations, it's likely not a universal truth.

---

14 Casper has since opened retail stores in select markets. However, the point remains: The company challenged an industry "absolute" by launching with a direct-to-consumer model—and it worked. That success paved the way for expansion into physical retail while still allowing the company to bypass the need for third-party showrooms. Casper's stores sell only Casper products, allowing them to retain full control over the customer experience.

In the 1960s, one such absolute dominated the world of adhesives: *The stronger, the better.* So when 3M scientist Spencer Silver set out to develop a new adhesive for aircraft construction, strength was his goal. But instead he created something that defied that logic: a weak, low-tack adhesive. It could stick lightly to other surfaces, peel away cleanly, and be reused without damage.

If considered only in its original context, that adhesive wouldn't have been a success. However, years later, another 3M scientist, Arthur Fry, applied that same adhesive in a completely different context—as a way to keep bookmarks in place without leaving any residue behind. That breakthrough led to the introduction of one of the most iconic stationery products of all time: the Post-it Note. An idea that didn't work in one context became a massive success in another—proof that testing absolutes across environments can reveal hidden pathways.

As you think about your own goals, consider whether your approach, product, or idea might thrive in unexpected contexts. Are you limiting yourself by targeting only one audience or applying your efforts to just one area? Just as 3M found unexpected value by thinking about adhesives in a different context—one where *weak* is actually better than *strong*—you might discover that what you're pursuing has broader applications than you initially imagined. Test your assumptions in new environments, and you may uncover untapped opportunities or alternative pathways to success.

Fourth, turn rules into tools. Rules, limitations, and restrictions often appear to be rigid absolutes, but they can also be manipulated to work in your favor. Hackers take rules to their logical extremes to see whether they can identify an advantage.

In the board game world, there's a term for people who meticulously study rules and use them in unexpected ways: *rules lawyers.* They don't break the rules, but they exploit technicalities, contradictions, and overlooked details to gain an edge. Even children instinctively test restrictions. If a parent says "no more talking," a child might respond by meowing, clapping, or using exaggerated gestures—because technically, those actions aren't talking.

Hackers take the same mindset and apply it to systems, policies, and processes, often turning restrictions into advantages. If a system has strict limitations, they might try to use those constraints to create a loophole. If there's a rule that dictates what must happen in a system, they might look for a way to use that requirement against the system.

In your own personal or work life, look for situations in which rules or constraints might contain hidden opportunities. Instead of seeing a restriction as a dead end, treat it as a creative challenge. Can you find a way to use the rules of a system *against* it? Are there rigid policies that lead to absurd or unintended results when followed literally? Testing absolutes doesn't always mean breaking the rules—it often means playing by them in a way that no one else has thought of.

After you've tested an absolute and found cases in which it is in fact not universally true, you can dig into those cases to find alternative ways of pursuing your goal.[15]

TACTIC #4 Reflect.

Hackers tend to be introspective, thoughtful, intentional people. They continuously evaluate their own skills, performance, and tactics. They push to improve every day. That pursuit necessarily

---

15 As a reminder, there are templates, guides, and additional exercises to help you implement this and other tactics mentioned throughout this book. You'll find them all listed in the appendix. You can certainly complete these exercises without them, but they're there to help you if you need them!

requires them to reflect on what's working, what's not, and what needs to change.

Reflection is a crucial part of the hacker experience and a powerful tool for identifying assumptions so that you can challenge them. When you succeed at something, analyze what worked and why. When you fail at something, analyze what didn't work and why. No matter what happens—win or lose—if you are constantly reflecting, you're constantly growing.

I recommend journaling daily. Journaling is a way to get to know yourself better, explore your thought patterns, observe your self-limiting beliefs, and understand your emotions. Taking time to reflect helps you understand why you think the way you do and how your thinking influences your behavior. In the process, your underlying assumptions reveal themselves—and then you can test them.

Here are a few good prompt questions to help you reflect on and then challenge assumptions:

- What do I believe about *X*?

- Why do I believe that?

- Has that belief proved to be true? If so, when and how?

- Has it ever proved to be false? If so, when and how?

- Do I want to change that belief? Why or why not?

As you ponder the moment of change that you're currently going through, journal about those questions. Find a quiet place free from the distractions of technology, family, work, and other interruptions. Let yourself relax into the experience and write whatever comes to mind. Periodically review what you've written in prior sessions. The combination of those two actions—writing and then later reading what you wrote—should reveal assumptions. Once you've identified those assumptions, you can challenge them.

TACTIC #5 **Stress test.**

Once you've identified your assumptions, put them under pressure—*on purpose.* Think of it like this: When engineers design a bridge, they don't just build it and hope for the best. They have it tested. They simulate extreme conditions such as excessive weight, heavy wind, or earthquakes. Then they see where it holds and where it cracks. They ask themselves, Can this thing survive under strain? Or will it collapse when reality hits?

Now apply that same mindset to your assumptions. Imagine you're a hacker. But instead of breaking into a software system, you'll be breaking into your own thinking. Hackers look for system weaknesses such as hidden faults, flawed logic, and rules that can be easily bypassed. That's your job here. You're going to poke holes in your thinking, push the limits of your assumptions, and ask uncomfortable questions. Your goal is not to throw everything out but to find what's *actually strong*—and what isn't.

Pick an assumption of yours and ask yourself a few questions:

- Is it possible that this assumption is wrong?
  If so, what would that mean?

- Is there a scenario in which the assumption absolutely must be true without exception?

- If there are exceptions to the assumption, what are they?

- If this assumption is true, can it be used to my advantage?

You can sort the assumptions you've identified into three groups: valid, flawed, and invalid. Hackers excel at this. They observe the assumptions that have been made and explore whether those assumptions are valid. Hackers understand that even valid assumptions often have weaknesses, and they look for those too.

Valid assumptions are the ones you've challenged and confirmed to be true. If you did not find any issues with an assumption, it's valid. That's great; there's clarity in confirmation. Now you can continue to operate under those valid assumptions *intentionally* rather than by default.

Flawed assumptions are mostly valid but have some problem with them. For example, maybe a process will take more time or less time than you assumed it would, but otherwise, your assumption about it is mostly true.

Invalid assumptions are completely wrong. For example, say you assumed that achieving a certain goal would require you to obtain a certain professional certification, but it turns out that it would not. In that case, your assumption would be invalid.

Flawed and invalid assumptions show you exactly where you can find new pathways. Explore those areas. Identify at least one new action you can take. Ask yourself what you can do differently now that you've observed where your assumptions are flawed or wrong.

Even correct assumptions can point you toward new pathways—especially when paired with flawed or overlooked ones.

Consider Chris, a hacker at ISE who worked at a technical support call center before joining our team. His previous workplace required employees to use a web application to request breaks. Only a limited number of "break slots" were available at any given time, and if no slots were open, the system would disable the "Start Break" button until one became available. The process created frantic races, with everyone staring at the screen, ready to click the button the moment a slot opened.

Assumptions

- **Valid** — Confirmation is clarity
- **Flawed**
- **Invalid** — Where to find new pathways!

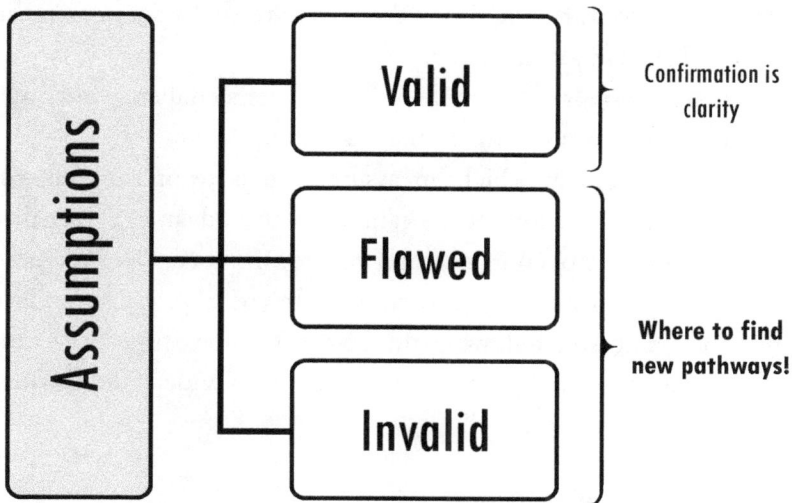

Instead of playing the same game as everyone else, Chris recognized two key assumptions:

1. An employee must wait until a slot opens to start a break (a valid assumption).

2. The "Start Break" button is disabled when no slots are available (a flawed assumption).

The first assumption was valid—once all slots were taken, no one else could take a break until one opened. But the second assumption was flawed. When a slot became available, there was a microscopic delay while the system verified the slot's availability before enabling the "Start Break" button. The button *appeared* disabled during that momentary gap. Chris figured out how to keep the button enabled so that he could click it the instant a slot became free—beating everyone else to it. By the time others were ready to pounce on the button, Chris had already clicked it.

That story is a great example of how hackers challenge assumptions to uncover ways to manipulate a system.

Look for cases in which an assumption is technically correct but still leaves room for you to gain a creative advantage. Say that something must happen in a certain way, for instance. Does the process rely on an unnecessary restriction? Can you bypass a secondary limitation while still following the core rule? Sometimes, the best exploits require us not to break the system but to understand its rules better than anyone else.

TACTIC #6 Reject norms.

When you challenge your assumptions, you question the underlying beliefs and accepted truths that guide your thinking and decision-making process. The act encourages critical thinking and helps you examine the rationale behind conventional wisdom. It forces you to ask probing questions that may lead you to uncover hidden biases or limitations. It is one of the ways that hackers find overlooked flaws that could result in catastrophic security breaches if exploited. It is a way that you can overcome complacency and embrace new perspectives.

You can take the idea even further by not only challenging assumptions but also rejecting norms. Rejecting norms involves *consciously refusing* to conform to established conventions or societal expectations. It entails breaking free from the constraints of tradition or conformity and charting your own path. Rejecting norms is a courageous and transformative act. It empowers you to define success on your own terms and pioneer new approaches. As one hacker once told me, "There's the normal way of doing things, and there's the abnormal way of doing things. Start with the first, but definitely try the second."

If you walk the halls of a hacker convention, at some point you'll probably see a guy or two with a mohawk haircut (dyed a bright color like pink or blue) wearing a utility kilt.[16] Outside those halls, in "regular" society, that aesthetic might be perceived as unusual, strange, or even weird. However, the kind of guy willing to reject norms to the point of wearing a utility kilt simply does not care about regular society's perceptions. That person is willing to reject societal norms and embrace their individuality. I've always admired that.

In *Hackable*, my first book, I included an entire section about what happens when you reject norms related to creating budget requests. I wanted to address a burning question that I hear all the time: How do I get appropriate funding approved for my cybersecurity budget? That is a very real, very difficult problem for many executives. Most executives justify their budget requests in a proven way—by citing risk-related considerations, compliance requirements, cost avoidance, threat trends, or cyber insurance requirements, for instance. However, there is a better way that is also a lot simpler: basing the argument on easy-to-understand metrics such as revenue, technology spend, or the size of the company or security team. That strategy represents a divergence from the norm, but it works.[17]

Here is a simple three-step process for rejecting a norm. First, identify the norm. Second, examine why the norm exists and why

---

16 A utility kilt is like a traditional kilt you'd see in Scotland but is made of durable materials like waxed denim or leather and has pockets similar to those found on cargo pants. They look badass, to be honest.

17 You can find a thorough discussion of this important topic in *Hackable*, and I've also included the related excerpt in the downloadable content for this book. Find that content at https://tedharrington.com/more.

people follow it. Third, determine whether the norm is worth rejecting—that is, whether it is safe for you to reject the norm and whether doing so will allow you to embrace independent thinking.

Through the courageous act of daring to be different, you will find overlooked pathways that the masses fail to notice.

TACTIC #7 Make it a lifetime practice.

Challenging assumptions isn't a onetime exercise. Like much of what you'll learn in this book, it's a *way of life*. It's a mindset that you'll return to over and over again. It's something you'll do regularly, maybe even every single day. The goal is to build a lifetime practice of identifying and then challenging the assumptions that shape your thinking. If you don't, your thinking may stagnate; you may develop gaps in your thinking that will cause you to miss opportunities.

Here's why making it an ongoing practice matters.

First, your views will inevitably change (or at least they should). What you believed ten years ago isn't necessarily what you believe now—and that's a good thing. New experiences, knowledge, and perspectives shape how we think. If you never challenge your assumptions, you risk clinging to outdated ideas just because they feel familiar.

Second, the world around you will change as well. Industries will transform, technology will advance, and social norms will evolve. What worked yesterday might be irrelevant tomorrow.

Third, it prevents intellectual laziness. The human brain defaults to pattern recognition. It helps us navigate life efficiently but also makes us overconfident in our assumptions. If you never challenge yourself, you'll stop questioning, and once you've stopped questioning, you'll stop learning.

Fourth, a lifelong commitment to challenging assumptions makes you more adaptable (a theme we will explore later in this book). People who thrive in uncertain, fast-changing environments are people who can quickly update their thinking. Challenging assumptions isn't about doubting everything—it's about staying open to better information and adjusting when needed.

Fifth, it gives you a competitive edge that sharpens over time. When it comes to creativity, problem-solving, and innovation, great ideas often come from the reconsideration of old assumptions. Hackers succeed because they question how things are supposed to work and find new unexpected pathways. By challenging assumptions when others unwittingly accept them, you'll continually expand your advantage: You'll be more likely to uncover new or better solutions, spot opportunities early, and approach problems from angles that others have never even considered.

Sixth, it helps you thwart the relentless creep of cognitive biases. We all fall victim to mental shortcuts like confirmation bias (seeing only evidence that supports our existing beliefs) and the sunk cost fallacy (sticking with bad decisions because we've already invested in them). But those biases don't just strike once—they appear repeatedly. They are insidious and inevitable; left unchecked, they'll undermine your progress. By challenging your assumptions regularly, you'll stay mentally sharper, see reality more clearly, and make better decisions throughout your life.

Seventh, it leads to ongoing personal growth. The biggest mental, emotional, and professional breakthroughs come from the realization that what you once thought was true...isn't. But that growth doesn't come from a single "aha" moment—it comes from the habit of questioning. If you're not revisiting your assumptions over time, you're probably not evolving.

In short, make challenging your assumptions a lifelong practice. Keep asking questions. Keep testing. Keep updating your thinking. Build a mindset of not accepting the world as it is but constantly exploring what it *could* be.

QUICK RECAP

▶ Conformist thinking means trusting assumptions without questioning them. Challenging those assumptions reveals the flaws they contain.

▶ To challenge your assumptions, you must first identify your assumptions.

▶ Implement the following tactics: ask other people, listen to understand, test absolutes, reflect, stress test, reject norms, and make it a lifetime practice.

For templates, exercises, and other tools to help you apply this, visit https://tedharrington.com/more.

Hackers are non-conforming,[18] and the first crucial step to embodying that trait is challenging assumptions. Now that you've learned how to apply the idea, let's talk about when, why, and how to break the rules.

---

18 You may have noticed that I'm using "non-conforming" instead of the more common variation, "nonconforming." That's intentional. I made that choice partly to provide a mnemonic for the traits of the hacker mindset: "the four Cs" (curious, non-conforming, committed, and creative). But more importantly, I did it because there's power in being non-conforming about how I choose to spell "non-conforming." Consider that a lesson in this crucial mindset trait.

CHAPTER 4

BREAK THE RULES

Conformist thinking means simply following the rules. Breaking the right ones reveals better ways to reach your goals.

Your whole life, you've been told to follow the rules.

"Obey the speed limit."

"Wait in line."

"Listen to your teachers."

"Sit down."

"Be quiet."

Well, I'm here to tell you that in some cases, you can break the rules. In fact, in certain cases, you *must* break the rules.

A rule specifies what is permitted, prohibited, or required in a given system. In computer systems, rules are important because they maintain stability and govern how those systems behave. In life, rules are important because they maintain order and govern how people behave.

Some rules are permissive, meaning they allow something (for example, freedom of speech). Others are restrictive, meaning they disallow something (for example, killing your neighbor). Some are both. (For example, freedom *of* religion also means freedom *from* religion—that is, you can practice your own faith, and no one else can impose their faith on you.)

However, rules are sometimes flawed. A rule that was created with good intentions may fail in execution. What you have to realize—and what hackers already know—is that in that disconnect lies opportunity.

Let's consider passwords for a moment. Passwords are a pain. Nevertheless, you need to deal with them, and you need to do so in the *right* way.

That means using long, complex, unique passwords. Let's break that down.

- A password should be long because each character exponentially increases the computational power required for an attacker to crack it.

- A password should be complex because the more variables (i.e., types of characters) a password has, the more computational power an attacker will need to crack it.

- A password should be unique so that if it is compromised by an attacker, the attacker will be unable to use it to gain access to other accounts too.

If you're like me, you probably can't remember more than a few passwords at a time. The good news is that there's an easy solution to that problem: using a password manager.

A password manager is a computer program that enables users to store and retrieve their passwords. When you use a password manager, you need to remember only a single password (the master password, used to log in to the password manager); the application saves the others for you. Password managers make it easier to use long, complex, unique passwords by simplifying the management of those passwords.

Pretty neat, right? You should definitely use one.

Which is why we needed to hack them.

We wanted to know whether attackers could extract secrets from password managers. So, our team of hackers set out to study four of the most popular password managers: LastPass, 1Password, Dashlane, and KeePass. The goal was to determine whether the passwords they store could be stolen (and if so, how to prevent that from happening). We wanted to see whether we could manipulate the systems to force them to expose users' secrets.

We set out to answer three questions:

1. Did we find any issues?

2. If so, did we publish our findings?

3. If so, did anything change as a result?

A "yes" to the first meant we'd uncovered something scientifically important. A second "yes" meant we'd done our part to bring that truth to light. And the third? That's the hardest outcome to achieve—and the entire point of doing research like this in the first place. It was the one we cared about most.

Pause to consider what this project meant: There are rules about how password managers work, rules about how they keep secrets safe, and rules about how users are supposed to interact with them. Our goal was to break *all* of those rules.

The project had three phases, each of which focused on a different system state:

1. Not running

2. Running and unlocked

3. Running and locked

First, we examined the applications without launching them, in what we referred to as the "not running" state. And things looked really good! We couldn't find a way for attackers to steal credentials or other sensitive information from a password manager in the "not running" state.

After that, though...yikes.

Next, we examined the systems in the "running and unlocked" state, meaning that a user has launched and logged in to a password manager and is actively using it. Through a combination of techniques such as keylogging, clipboard sniffing, and binary modification, we found several ways to extract a user's primary password (the password for the password manager itself) and steal other secrets.[19]

---

19 Don't worry about the technical details mentioned above. They're included here merely as a way to illustrate the problem and our work, but you don't need to understand the specifics in order to extract the key lessons from the story. (That being said, if you work in tech or cybersecurity and want to do some further reading on the technical details, you can find them at https://tedharrington.com/more.)

That was a bad thing.

The central promise of a password manager is that it will keep your secrets, well, *secret*. Our research proved otherwise. We showed how the rules could be broken and how all of the treasure could be stolen when they were.

In the third phase, things got even worse. We looked at the password managers in the "running and locked" state, the state that exists after a user has launched, logged in to, and logged out of a password manager (or has launched but not logged in to it). Theoretically, the state should have had the same security posture as the first state studied in our research (the "not running" state).

Unfortunately, that wasn't the case. Even in the "running and locked" state, several of the systems exposed a way for attackers to extract users' primary passwords (and other secrets too). In fact, *all* of the password managers we examined allowed the trivial extraction of at least some secrets.

Applications that *we weren't even logged in to* were giving up the crown jewels. That meant that the secrets of up to 60 million users were vulnerable to exposure *even when the applications were in a locked state*.

Password manager research	
Phase/state	**Result**
Not running	Good!
Running and unlocked	Bad.
Running and locked	Catastrophic!

Table 3. The phases of our research and their results (simplified)

What happened next illustrates exactly why breaking the rules is *sometimes* a good thing.

When we concluded our research, we went through the responsible disclosure process, in which security researchers share their findings on a system with the affected company or organization so that it can fix the system's problems. Then we worked with *The Washington Post* to write an exclusive exposé on our research.[20]

There was a lot of commotion after that. Our team was invited to speak at conferences. We appeared on podcasts. We wrote articles. The most interesting outcome occurred a few days after the story broke, when we received a phone call from the chief technology officer (CTO) of a company whose password manager had *not* been included in the research.

"Why didn't you include us?" the executive asked.

When you think about it, that was a funny reaction to a news story about companies whose tech could be hacked. Why would you want to be in that story? Well, the CTO wanted to be included because the research resonated with them.

"Security is the main promise we make to our users," the CTO explained. "We'd love to know what our issues are. We'd love to fix them. We'd love the world to know that we are constantly improving."

We all smiled at that. The *entire purpose* of security research is to make things better. We had invested half a year in our project, redirected focus from other projects, and spent a substantial amount of money on pursuing the effort. It had been worth it.

We returned to our threefold definition of success:

1.   Had we found any issues? *Check.*

---

20   If you want to read it, you can find a link to the original story at https://tedharrington.com/more.

2. Had we disclosed and then published our findings? *Check.*

3. Had our research made an impact? *Check.*

We found flaws that could have harmed users.[21] We helped the affected companies improve their tech. We reached a worldwide audience by publishing our results. The work resonated with other uninvolved companies that wanted to improve too.

We achieved all of those outcomes because we were willing to explore how to bend, break, and bypass rules. Pretty much every project that ethical hackers work on requires them to look at rules, examine how they function and why they function that way, and explore how they can be bent, broken, or bypassed. Attackers do that too, but they *don't care* that they're breaking the rules.

That is important, so let me repeat it: *Attackers do not care about the rules.*

That's exactly why ethical hacking matters. Rules can—and will—be broken. The only questions are *how*, and what will happen when they are. Sometimes it leads to chaos. Sometimes, it leads to insight. When the rules of a computer system are bypassed, all kinds of unexpected outcomes become possible—some dangerous, others illuminating.

And the same thing is true in life.

When you start looking at the rules you've been following—the ones you've never questioned—you'll start to see which ones are holding you back. Break the right ones, and suddenly you'll find

---

21 There is a technique for ensuring that even if your password manager account is hacked, your passwords won't be compromised. Find a step-by-step guide to implementing that technique in the bonus content available at https://tedharrington.com/more.

the shortcuts, loopholes, and unexpected pathways that will get you further, faster.

Observing This Mindset in the Real World

If you want to win, sometimes you have to bend the rules.

Years ago, one of our software developers, James, found himself on a senior class trip to a historically preserved island in Lake Michigan. The class was broken up into small teams, each of which was equipped with an instant film camera to be used in a scavenger hunt. The teams had to find items that were located all around the island and take a picture in front of each one. The first team to take pictures of all of them would win.

The island itself is pretty large, and there were no motorized vehicles on it. The options for getting around were renting bicycles or going on foot. Almost every team opted to rent bicycles. After all, the scavenger hunt spanned miles, and winning would require speed.

James's team, however, opted not to rent bikes. He and his teammates chose to do the contest entirely on foot. They made that decision partly because they wanted to save money and partly because they wanted the challenge. They wanted to see whether they could compete despite the disadvantage.

Racing on foot against competitors on bicycles inherently changes the way you think about the game itself. James and his teammates knew they wouldn't be able to outrun bicycles, so they'd have to outthink the bikers. To do that, they thought strategically about the puzzle-like aspects of the scavenger hunt. They identified items that might be near one another and considered how to pursue each group of items to minimize their travel time. They optimized their approach for speed and efficiency.

For much of the competition, their strategy worked. Despite

its mobility disadvantage, James's team kept pace with its bicycle-advantaged opponents. However, when it came time to hunt for the final item, it became clear that they were going to lose. They were on the eastern edge of the island, and the final item was located on the western edge. It would have taken about fifteen minutes to get there by bike but would take at least forty-five minutes if they ran, which some team members weren't capable of doing anyway. They were exhausted from running around all day, and their opponents were already en route to the final clue. There was just no way they could physically pull it off.

They had to find another way.

James understood the reality of the competitive situation.

"Let's think about this," he told his teammates. "We aren't going to win on foot." His teammates agreed.

So instead of running, they started brainstorming.

Suddenly, an idea struck. The final item they needed to find was part of the most iconic site on the historic island: a bridge.

"What if…" James started. "What if we found another way to get a picture in front of it?" He explained his idea: There was a tourist kiosk very close to their current location, and surely there would be a picture of the bridge at that kiosk. What if they took a picture of themselves not in front of the *actual* site but in front of a *picture* of it?

They looked at the scavenger hunt rule book to see what it said. It turned out that the rules weren't clear on the point. The book said only that the teams needed pictures of themselves in front of each item. James's team felt that the *intent* of the rule was likely to get the teams to take pictures in front of the actual items. However, the *letter* of the rule—the actual wording of it—left room for a different interpretation.

They discussed the possibility that their plan could disqualify them. They felt that the risk was worth it: They weren't going to win on foot, and the rules didn't seem to expressly prohibit their plan. So they made the decision to take the risk and accept the outcome—either winning or disqualification.

Then James and his team walked over to the tourist kiosk, found a picture of the iconic site, took a photo of themselves in front of it, and went to relax in the shade at the nearby finish line.

Over an hour later, the other teams started to arrive. One by one, the members of those teams stared in wide-eyed disbelief at James and his team just chilling there, relaxed and obviously done with the hunt.

"Did you guys quit?!" the others would ask.

"Nope, we finished over an hour ago!" James and his teammates would reply.

When it came time to name a winner, there was quite a commotion. Every other team felt that James's team had cheated. James and his teammates pointed out that the language of the rules didn't prohibit what they'd done.

Their strategy was definitely in a gray area, so the decision came down to a judgment call by the chaperone. The chaperone was in a good mood and decided that he loved the creative solution to the problem. He named James's team the winner.

He and his teammates took a risk, and they won because they were willing to look closely at the rules and explore how to break, bypass, or bend them. Other people might not have liked their approach, but it helped James and his teammates achieve their goal—and do it a *lot* faster than everyone else.

That's the hacker ethos.

How to Apply This to Your Life

Ethical hackers excel at questioning the rules of computer systems—often by breaking them. That same mindset fosters independent thinking and innovation in everyday life. Here's how you can stay skeptical of the rules while still honoring legality and morality.

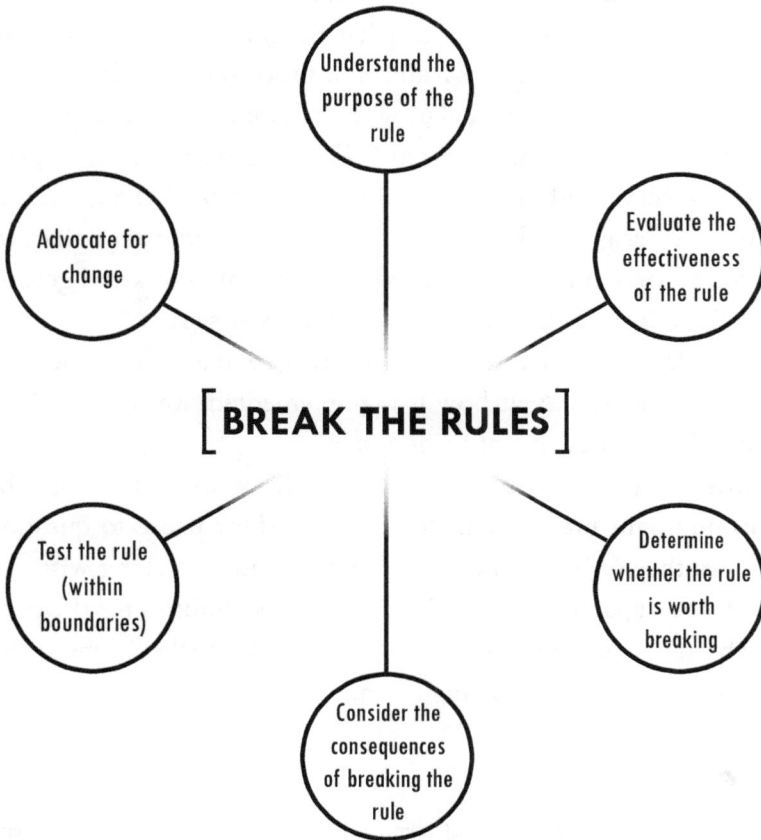

Understand the purpose of the rule

Evaluate the effectiveness of the rule

Advocate for change

[BREAK THE RULES]

Test the rule (within boundaries)

Determine whether the rule is worth breaking

Consider the consequences of breaking the rule

`TACTIC #1` Understand the purpose of the rule.

You learned in chapter 1 that hackers ask why, and that concept applies to rules, too. To bypass the rules that could prevent them from achieving their goals, hackers first seek to understand why those rules exist. Hackers know that grasping the reason a rule was developed and implemented in the first place will help them figure out whether the rule is valid and how they can bypass it if it's not.

At ISE, whenever we find ourselves in the early stages of a security assessment, scoping out what the project might entail, we explore why certain security features or processes exist. That is crucial because there is often a glaring discrepancy between *why* a rule exists and *how* it is implemented.[22] Focusing on what a company aims to achieve with a system helps us understand the reasoning behind the design of its security controls. If we understand that, we can concentrate on the company's ultimate goals and avoid getting sidetracked by less critical details of its security setup.

If we don't seek to understand the purpose of a security measure and instead look only at how it is implemented, we might miss a glaring flaw in the logic of its design.

Most people who make rules don't think about how or why someone might break them. Most people don't pause to question the rules they've been asked to follow; they just go along with the crowd. The gaps in their thinking create opportunities for the people who do consider those things—people like hackers, who question the rules before following them.

---

22   This is a key concept that many companies get wrong. You can satisfy every control in a compliance program and still not be secure. Compliance frameworks are designed to be broadly applicable, but they can't account for every organization's unique risks and context. It's possible to check every box and still miss the point.

A well-implemented security measure is useless if it secures the wrong thing in the wrong way. Hackers seek to understand the purpose of a system's rules so that they can evaluate whether the rules are valid.

The same idea applies to your life too. As you pursue your goals, there will be rules that govern certain aspects of your approach. Examine why those rules exist so that you can then determine whether and how to bypass the ones that are nonsensical.

When you encounter a rule, consider who made the rule and why. What was their motivation? What were they trying to protect, restrict, or allow? Why?

For example, have you ever noticed that when you are checking out of a retail store, the clerk usually asks for your phone number and email address? Most people just automatically provide that information because doing so feels like a required part of the transaction. Have you ever paused and asked the clerk, "Do you need this information?" That's what I do, and every time the answer is no. I understand the purpose of the "rule": The store is simply looking to collect information on its customers. It is not crucial to the completion of the transaction. I don't have any issue with a company wanting to know its customers; I just don't feel like wasting time spelling out my long and complicated contact information, especially when it does not benefit me. I just want to pay for my items and leave.

By contrast, I belong to a gym that asks you to avoid putting weights on the floor during your workout. The gym wants you to place them on specialized stands or pads on the floor. That is very unusual. Normally, you do your repetitions, put the weights on the floor while you rest, and then pick them up for the next set. I've never seen another gym enforce such a rule. In fact, some gyms even *encourage* members to throw their weights down after a lift! (If you've ever been near a CrossFit gym, you've likely heard the loud crashes that come with it.)

I love this gym, so when I first learned about the rule, I tried my best to follow it. However, I kept forgetting about it because I didn't understand why it was necessary. No other gym had ever required me to follow that rule, so it felt arbitrary. As a result, I kept absent-mindedly putting weights on the floor. The staff was nice about it but kept reminding me of the rule. Eventually, I decided to ask why the rule existed. I needed to understand its purpose. It turned out that the gym is located directly above apartments, and dropping weights on the floor rattles the homes below. Once I learned that the rule was about being considerate to neighbors, it took on a whole new meaning. From that moment on, I never forgot where to put my weights.

Understand the reasoning behind the rule you're considering, because it will likely reveal whether you should honor the rule at all. You may find that there are ways to meet the spirit of the rule without following it to the letter.

TACTIC #2 Evaluate the effectiveness of the rule.

After considering the purpose of a rule, assess whether the rule achieves its intended purpose. This tactic gets to the core of hacking: questioning assumptions and validating the ways that things actually work. Security issues often arise when systems don't function as people believe they do—when there's a gap between perception and reality. That's especially true when it comes to rules.

I was recently at the airport for a flight to Portugal, flying with an airline I'd never used before. Despite being a seasoned traveler, I was unfamiliar with the airline's baggage rules. I learned I could bring a personal item but not my rolling carry-on. Annoying, but fine—I'd just check the bag. Then came the twist: The weight limit for checked luggage was a mere 8 kilograms, and my bag weighed 11.5 kilograms. That seemed absurdly low, but rules are rules, so I asked about the fee for an overweight bag. $150! Preposterous.

Sensing my frustration, the agent suggested I shift some weight from my carry-on to my personal item. Equally absurd, but fine—I complied. So there I was, kneeling on the airport floor, sweating from effort and embarrassed by the spectacle I was creating, shoveling clothes between bags while trying to ignore the sharp stares of other passengers. After a while, the agent stopped me with a smile and said, "That's good enough. You've shown that you tried." My bag, then 9.2 kilograms, was still overweight, but she checked it without charging me the fee.

As I walked away, frustrated and bewildered, I couldn't help but ask myself a question: What had the airline actually accomplished there? The purpose of a weight limit is to keep the plane light enough to control its fuel costs, which in turn keeps fares reasonable—goals I fully support. But the airline's rule didn't serve those goals. All 11.5 kilograms were still on the plane, just split between the cargo hold and the cabin. And the weight limit was "satisfied" not through actual compliance but through the mere appearance of effort. Those facts were clear signs that the rule was ineffective (and in my opinion, outright ludicrous).

As you work toward your goals, you'll encounter rules that, though well intentioned, are poorly implemented or downright absurd. Keep an eye out for them—they often reveal overlooked opportunities.

Here's a simple three-step process for evaluating the effectiveness of a rule.

First, observe the rule in action. Pay attention to how the rule is applied in real-world scenarios. In our luggage example, that would involve going through the process of checking bags and noting what happened under various conditions, such as a bag being underweight or overweight.

Second, compare the outcome to the purpose. Determine whether the rule's results align with its intended goal. In the luggage example, the rule failed to reduce the overall weight that I brought on board, missing its objective entirely.

Third, judge the rule's validity. If the rule's outcomes don't align with its purpose, the rule is invalid. The luggage policy, for instance, was invalid because its implementation failed to satisfy its goal.

Now simply replace the luggage example with whatever you're trying to achieve. The three-step process is applicable whether your goal is to obtain a raise, a new job, or venture capital funding—or really to do anything else.

Once you've determined that a rule is ineffective, the next step is to ask yourself what would *actually* accomplish the intended outcome. If a rule fails to achieve its goal, you may be able to find a better way to navigate the system. But recognizing that a rule is ineffective doesn't mean that you can ignore it outright. It means that first, you need to figure out whether there's a smarter way to achieve the goal despite the nonsense.

In the luggage example, complying with the *intention* of the rule rather than the letter of the rule saved me $150. In other situations, recognizing the ineffectiveness of a rule might help you get what you need faster with fewer obstacles or on more favorable terms.

Furthermore, if you realize that a rule is enforced inconsistently, you can use that knowledge to your advantage. Many rules—especially bureaucratic ones—are more about the *perception of effort* than actual compliance. When you understand that, you can focus on what really matters rather than following inefficient processes without questioning them. Whether you're negotiating a deal, securing a promotion, or navigating red tape, the principle remains the same:

Focus on what actually gets results, not just on what's written in the rule book.

TACTIC #3 **Determine whether the rule is worth breaking.**
Hackers tend to *question* every rule, but they don't *break* every rule. Breaking a rule can sometimes be inefficient, lead nowhere, or simply not be worth the effort. Knowing which rules are worth breaking is crucial because hackers, like all of us, have limited time, money, and energy. Those resources must be directed toward the areas in which they'll have the greatest impact.

Before we go further, let's acknowledge that most rules are valuable. Imagine a world with no traffic laws; it would be chaos. Rules create structure and safety. However, over time, many systems accumulate rules on top of rules. This phenomenon, called *rule bloat*, can create inefficiencies and unnecessary obstacles.

A great example of rule bloat is the manner in which most companies handle vacation time. Most companies have tons of rules related to paid time off: You have to accrue it, become eligible to use it, put in a request to *actually* use it, and get the request approved, to name just a few requirements. Meanwhile, the company has to track all related data in disparate software systems, report on it, and manage it. That's a lot of effort just to allow someone to go sit on the beach!

I come from a point of view devoted to looking out for the *bad* in the world, yet I have observed a powerful, perhaps surprising, truth: Most people are *good* people. Generally speaking, most people are kind and behave ethically in most situations.[23] Most people don't

---

23 Of course, there are exceptions. And to be clear, this isn't a statistically proven claim. It's just something I've observed to be true in my experience— and hopefully you have too.

abuse company policies. But because a small percentage of employees *do*, companies decide to implement strict rules that govern everyone's behavior. It's a pain in the ass and completely unnecessary.

Companies do not need to treat everyone like they're the harmful few. Instead, they should treat everyone like they can be trusted to do the right thing—that is, hire quality people, fire the toxic ones quickly, trust everyone to do their job, and remove the red tape that could prevent them from recharging when needed.[24] If the company culture is right, that way of thinking works. We have an unlimited vacation policy at ISE, and it's never been a problem. (I'm not saying you should necessarily break rules surrounding time off in your role; I'm just pointing those rules out as an example of bloat.)

The key to effective rule breaking lies in identifying unnecessary or redundant rules that when bypassed will move you closer to your goal. Although most rules exist to help a system operate properly, there are some that do the opposite. Unfortunately, distinguishing between beneficial rules and bloated ones isn't always an intuitive process. Here are three ways to tell which category a rule falls into.

First, consider its outcome. Does the rule directly contribute to the desired result? A beneficial rule has a clear positive impact on performance, productivity, or quality, while a bloated rule does not.

Second, consider its necessity. Is the rule necessary in many different scenarios, or does it apply only in rare cases? A beneficial rule works broadly; a bloated rule may be overly rigid or redundant.

---

24 By "trust," I mean letting good people do the job they were hired to do—without layering on bloated, unnecessary processes. That doesn't mean ignoring risk. The insider threat is real, and verification still matters. But once someone has earned trust, they should be empowered to work as efficiently as possible.

A beneficial rule...		A bloated rule...
• Achieves the desired outcomes		• Lacks positive impact
• Is consistent and necessary	vs.	• Is rarely needed
• Is flexible and adaptable		• Is overly rigid

Third, consider its flexibility and adaptability. Is it possible to adjust the rule to suit changing circumstances without sacrificing its effectiveness? A beneficial rule is adaptable; a bloated rule is inflexible and hinders responsiveness to change.

Let's contrast two widely implemented rules: don't kill and don't jaywalk.

For the purpose of this analysis, let's ignore the extreme disparities in their moral implications and consequences. Let's focus just on examining them in terms of our three criteria for judging whether a rule is beneficial.

"Don't kill" is a beneficial rule because it achieves the desired outcome of keeping society safe. It's also consistently necessary. At the same time, it is adaptable and flexible—killing can be necessary at times. Wars, murder trials, and even suffering pets sometimes justify the act.

By contrast, "don't jaywalk" is a bloated rule. It only sort of achieves the dual goal of ensuring the safety of pedestrians and maintaining the flow of vehicle traffic. It's not always necessary, even in dense and busy urban areas. Furthermore, it's not really adaptable. For example, prohibiting jaywalking at busy intersections is reasonable, but the rule definitely doesn't matter when it comes to quiet side streets. Technically, though, the rule is the same in both scenarios.

Perhaps not all rules will be as glaringly distinct as the ones we've just contrasted, but hopefully, the example illustrates the point.

Once you've identified a bloated rule, determine whether it is worth breaking. The breaking of a rule should deliver a clear benefit to you, others, or society. Ask yourself the following questions to assess the merits of bypassing a rule:

- Does the rule create obstacles that slow your progress toward your goal?

- Would bypassing the rule help you achieve your goal faster?

- Could breaking the rule enable you to achieve your goal on a larger scale or in a more impactful way?

- Would bypassing the rule remove unnecessary frustrations or inefficiencies?

- Could breaking the rule save you critical resources such as time, money, or energy?

- Is it possible to bypass the rule without violating ethical standards?

If you answered yes to at least half of those questions, you've likely found a rule worth breaking. As always, trust your instincts and be ethical.

TACTIC #4 **Consider the consequences of breaking the rule.**
The decision of whether to break a rule is a matter of risk analysis.

It's critical to weigh the potential benefits of breaking a rule against the risks and consequences. Ethical hackers understand that and are accustomed to carefully considering the consequences of rule breaking in their work.

When hackers are contracted to perform security testing for a company, the rules are clear. They're paid to attempt to bypass the system constraints, rules, or security measures within a defined project scope. And as long as they act legally, ethically, and in adherence with the contract's terms, their rule breaking poses little to no risk to them. It's their job.

But ethical hacking isn't always contractual. Ethical hackers sometimes look for vulnerabilities in a system as part of security research, in which case norms and laws rather than contracts dictate what they can and cannot do. For instance, probing a proprietary system for flaws is often permissible, but exploiting those flaws is not. The goal of ethical hacking is to improve security, not harm it. Moreover, an ethical hacker who violates a boundary may face consequences such as reputational damage or legal penalties (even jail time) depending on the severity of the violation.

Malicious hackers also consider the consequences of their actions—but through a different lens. They strategize to minimize risk, using tactics such as operating out of countries without extradition treaties or collecting ransoms in cryptocurrency to avoid detection and intervention by law enforcement. They know their actions could carry heavy penalties, so they build their methods around the goal of evading capture.

The lesson here isn't to calculate the risks of engaging in illegal activities. You shouldn't do illegal things that harm people; I hope that's obvious. The point is to carefully evaluate the repercussions of bypassing a rule. In some cases, breaking a rule will have negligible consequences, but in others, it can lead to serious personal or societal harm. Avoid harming anyone—physically, emotionally, or metaphorically—including yourself. Focus on rules that can be broken with only minimal repercussions or on rules so harmful (e.g., so racist, sexist, or otherwise discriminatory) that their violation is justifiable even if it would carry significant risk.

Take Steve's experience at grad school, for example. It annoyed him that school security guards would make students show their IDs to enter a building but wouldn't actually look closely at those IDs. Steve's a curious guy (as hackers tend to be), and he wanted to explore that practice. He began to wonder whether he could enter buildings without providing his actual student ID. So he started experimenting with showing increasingly absurd alternatives to his ID. One day he flashed a guard his wallet without the ID. He was waved through. The next day, a random flyer. Same result. The next day he showed his gloves. Good to go. As long as he showed the guards something—literally *anything*—they let him through.

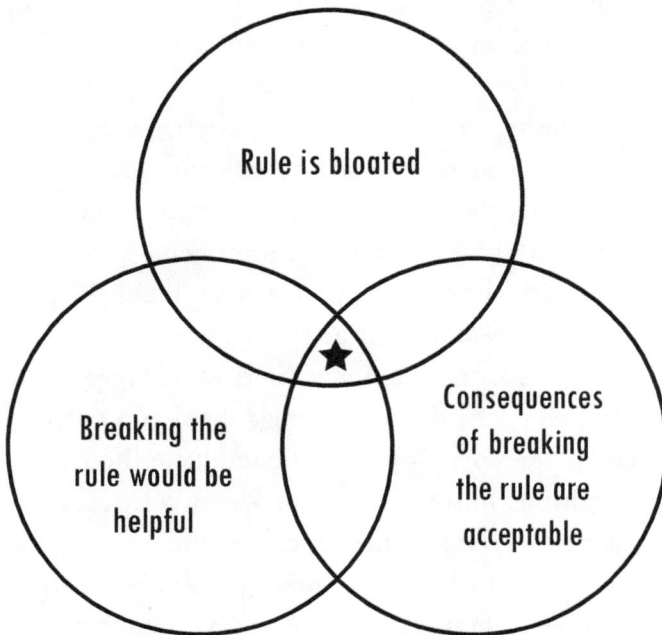

Rule is bloated

Breaking the rule would be helpful

Consequences of breaking the rule are acceptable

The key takeaway is that the consequences of bending that rule were negligible. At worst, he could have been stopped by a guard and asked to show his real ID before being allowed to walk into a building. Now imagine trying his experiment at a nuclear weapons facility in a country hostile to Americans. Those guards wouldn't laugh. The consequences would be severe and would likely include interrogation, jail time, torture, or worse. Same action—vastly different outcomes.

As you identify bloated rules that would be beneficial to break, pause to assess the consequences of doing so. If they would be minor, consider moving forward. If they would be severe, ensure the risk is truly worth the reward.

TACTIC #5 Test the rule (within boundaries).

We've identified three indications that a rule is worth breaking: (1) the rule is bloated, (2) breaking it would be helpful, and (3) the consequences of breaking it are acceptable. Once you've found a rule that meets those criteria, it's time to explore bypassing or breaking the rule.

It is essential to break rules within limits. (I acknowledge the absurdity of a rule about how to break rules. Just bear with me; this is important.) The underlying idea is simple: *Don't violate anyone, including yourself.* Here are specific boundaries that should be respected:

- **Ethical boundaries:** Act in ways that align with your core values and preserve your integrity. Breaking a rule isn't worth compromising who you are.

- **Safety boundaries:** Ensure the physical and psychological well-being of everyone involved. Don't put yourself or others in danger.

- **Reputational boundaries:** Protect your hard-earned reputation. Avoid actions that could damage your credibility or that of others.

- **Mission boundaries:** Ensure that your actions support your larger goals and objectives. Avoid distractions.

- **Legal boundaries:** Respect the role that legal restrictions play in a society. Laws generally exist to maintain order and fairness.

There is a caveat to that last point. While laws are typically meant to maintain order, not all laws are just. Certain laws perpetuate harm or inequality, and historically, breaking those laws has sometimes been necessary to the advancement of society. Consider the Underground Railroad, a clandestine network of supportive individuals who shepherded enslaved people from Southern states to the free North in nineteenth century America. The actions of those involved were illegal at the time, but morally and ethically, they were unequivocally right.

Generally speaking, don't break the law. In the rare case that breaking an unjust law will benefit society, you can consider doing so as long as you approach the decision thoughtfully and with a clear moral purpose.

With those boundaries in mind, let's explore how to break rules effectively.

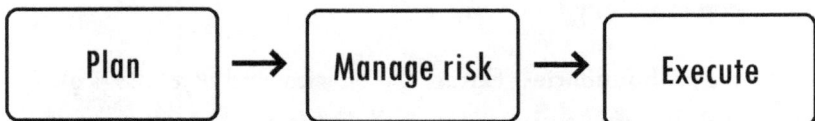

Plan → Manage risk → Execute

First, plan your approach. Develop a clear strategy. Identify specific steps, a timeline, and the necessary resources. Even if you'll be breaking a simple bureaucratic rule, planning your approach will minimize the likelihood of a mistake and ensure your success.

Second, mitigate and then accept the associated risks. The objective is to minimize the potential fallout of your rule breaking. Prepare a defense, rally your allies, and create a backup plan. Once you've done all that, accept that things might not go the way you planned. Ethical hackers often face some degree of risk, even when doing the work they've been hired to perform. For example, there was a high-profile situation in Iowa in which the state government hired a company to test the physical security of a courthouse. The company successfully breached the building, after which it followed the correct agreed-upon protocol: The company triggered an alarm to signal the completion of the project, and waited for the police to arrive. Despite having been contracted to perform the work, the testers were sent to jail, where they languished for weeks. The individuals who performed that work are still facing legal fallout many years later. That kind of outcome is rare, but it underscores the importance of managing the level of risk and accepting the fact that it's never zero.

Third, execute. When it's time to act, go all in. Avoid hesitation. Adapt if things go sideways. Breaking a rule is inherently stressful, but trust the preparation that you've done. Fully commit. As Yoda said, "Do or do not. There is no 'try.'"

TACTIC #6 Advocate for change.

The purpose of ethical hacking is to *make things better*. Hackers achieve that by doing two things: finding flaws and sharing them with the affected organization (and then, in some cases, with the world). Ideally, the affected organization will fix the issue, resulting in a better more secure system. That's progress, and progress is good.

Progress is not static, though. Nor is security. Security isn't something you achieve once and can then forget about. It's an ongoing process of improvement. It's about doing the work that will set you up for success tomorrow. Breaking the rules can be a powerful catalyst for progress. When rules are broken, new pathways emerge—ones that will make things better, faster, more efficient, more effective, and more profitable.

Progress also doesn't happen in isolation. It requires knowledge sharing. The discussions that follow the breaking of a rule are what drive progress. They are the reason that rules in sports evolve, laws change, and social norms shift.

That's why ethical hackers perform responsible disclosure. Finding vulnerabilities isn't enough—ethical hackers must share their findings so that they can be addressed. That's how things improve. That commitment to sharing their knowledge is also why hackers write white papers, deliver talks, and give interviews. It's why people like me write books. Sharing knowledge isn't just about pointing out flaws; it's about presenting solutions. It's about inspiring change.

Whenever you break a rule and achieve a positive outcome, share what you've learned. Help others who are facing similar challenges. Advocate for the better way you've discovered. What you've accomplished isn't theoretical. It's real progress. It's proof of a better path.

That being said, exercise discretion in deciding when and where you'll share your findings. Your rule breaking may piss people off, especially if they're personally invested in the rule you broke. Or maybe you need to reuse a work-around you discovered and don't want to see it closed off yet, which would likely occur if you disclosed it. Balance the societal benefit against the toll you might pay for being a champion for change. Ultimately, trust your instincts—just as hackers do.

Whenever you can, advocate for change. If not you, then who? If not now, then when?

Closing Caveat

Rules are often unclear.

Sometimes the intent and the application of a rule don't align with each other. Sometimes the world has changed so much that a rule no longer makes sense. Sometimes the consequences of a rule are unclear; perhaps the rule has never been tested before, and no one knows what will happen once the rule is broken.

Entire professions, such as the legal profession, exist to try to interpret what specific rules mean. If all rules were clear, lawyers wouldn't be necessary. Studying the rules can be a lifelong endeavor that may never lead to clarity.

The information in this chapter is not intended to be a substitute for law school, serve as legal advice, or be interpreted as the universal standard on rules or laws. The processes of making and breaking rules contain many nuances that a single chapter could not possibly fully explore.

What this chapter *is* intended to do is help you think critically about the rules that affect you so that you can find the ones worth breaking in a safe, ethical manner.

QUICK RECAP

▶ Conformist thinking means simply following the rules. Breaking the right ones reveals better ways to reach your goals.

▶ Find bloated rules worth breaking; then minimize the risks of breaking them and do so in ways that benefit you without harming others. Be careful to stay within appropriate boundaries, and do not violate anyone, including yourself.

▶ Implement the following tactics: understand the purpose of the rule, evaluate the effectiveness of the rule, determine whether the rule is worth breaking, consider the consequences of breaking the rule, test the rule (within boundaries), and advocate for change.

For templates, exercises, and other tools to help you apply this, visit https://tedharrington.com/more.

Now that you've explored why and how to break rules, let's explore the hacker superpower: asking "what if?"

CHAPTER 5

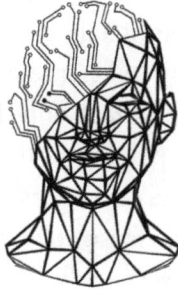

ASK "WHAT IF?"

Conformist thinking means accepting
things the way they are. Asking "what if?"
inspires new ways of thinking.

When a thirteen-year-old kid takes your entire system offline, it's a bad day.

My nephew used to love video games. In one of his favorite games, there are two different kinds of portals a player can jump through, each of which transports the player to a different place within the game. The gameplay itself isn't important, but this is: My nephew asked "what if" questions. Specifically, he wondered, *What if you put the portals directly on top of each other and sent a player through both at the same time?*

As it turns out, you'd completely crash the game.

The "portal trick" literally takes the entire game offline. It's not a console game, so it didn't affect only him. It is an *online* game. There were tons of people playing it all over the world. The game crashed for *everyone.* No one could play it at all. Tournaments were interrupted. Players became frustrated. The game stopped making money. Sponsors couldn't serve ads. The game developer couldn't sell in-game purchases.

The game was offline for a full five minutes—an eternity in online gaming. He sat there patiently, and when it came back online, he wondered…

Was that me?

Did I do that?

Crashing the game was not at all what he expected. However, he's a curious kid, and he wanted to explore this further. He wondered whether the crash had been just a fluke or something more serious. He didn't want to hurt anyone; he just wanted to know whether he'd stumbled upon a real problem.

So, he tried it again.

He placed one portal directly on top of the other and jumped his character into it.

Sure enough, it completely crashed the game. *Again.*

That's pretty wild when you think about it. He found a catastrophic security flaw simply by asking "what if?" He's not a trained security professional. He wasn't even an adult yet. Nevertheless, he found the kind of issue companies pay ethical hackers big money to find.

Fortunately for the game developers, he's a good kid with a strong sense of ethics. He knew exactly what to do and reported the vulnerability to them. He showed the developers what he'd done, the impact it had caused, and the process they could use to replicate the issue. He wanted to help them fix it so that it wouldn't become a problem for his friends, other players, or himself.

The developers thanked him for his help and fixed the issue.[25]

My nephew might not describe himself as a hacker, but the story is a vivid example of what hackers do. They probe, explore, and ask "what if?" Once they've found a potential issue, they investigate its exploitability. Then they help fix it (at least, the ethical ones do).

All of it starts with a question: "What if?"

That question unlocks the part of your brain that rejects norms, releases you from the shackles of the way you're "supposed" to do something, and enables you to think differently.

That shift in mindset—that's what hackers do. You can too.

Observing This Mindset in the Real World

"So I gotta ask you…"

On every ski trip, without fail, someone eventually approaches me with a question. It's always about the same thing: my ski poles. Or, I should say, my lack thereof.

You see, I ski without poles. That's unusual, at least at American resorts. Basically, the only people without ski poles are children… and me. It never fails to draw attention from other skiers.

In case you don't ski, here's a quick primer on the gear: You

---

25 I need to emphasize how awesome this company's response was! Many companies fail to do either or both of the following: (1) acknowledge reported security issues and (2) actually fix them. The game development company did both, and as a result, it has a more secure system. That's the whole point of security research—to make things better.

need a helmet to protect your head, technical clothing to keep you warm and dry, skis to glide down the mountain, boots to attach your feet to the skis, and poles to…well, actually, I'm not sure why you need poles.

One day, I found myself pondering that question. *Why do I need poles?*

I figured I was missing something, so I started asking everyone I could on the mountain—from skiers to ski patrol to ski instructors. Surprisingly, no one could give me a good answer. Literally everyone insisted I needed poles, but no one provided a reason that made sense to me.

Some people told me poles were essential for navigating moguls (technical terrain that requires you to make sharp pivots). I don't ski moguls often enough to justify carrying equipment specific to that terrain—but even if I did, I've observed that mogul experts don't use poles that way when they rip through mogul fields. Others said poles are helpful on flat terrain where you aren't being pulled downhill by gravity, but it's easier and faster to skate out of those areas using just your legs. A lot of people said poles are for balance, but that's just not true: I'm actually more balanced without them.

One ski instructor was so frustrated at *just being asked* that question that he threw up his hands and said, "I don't know what to tell you, Ted. Girls dig guys who ski with poles."

I laughed. He didn't.

By the end of that season, I'd heard from every perspective—novices to experts, guests to staff, and just about everyone in between. Yet no one had given me a solid reason why I needed poles. Poles come with a lot of hassle: They're just one more thing to carry, buy, maintain, damage, and lose. They complicate the process of loading and unloading chairlifts. Why deal with all that if there's no clear benefit?

So I paused to ask an important question:

What if I skied without poles?

I decided to experiment. One day, I left the poles back at the lodge, and something magical happened: I skied better than I ever had before. I felt so much more in tune with my body. My rhythm was a straight-up metronome. It felt like I was dancing as I zoomed down the mountain. My life was simpler with less gear. (And, as an unintended side benefit, my lack of poles was a fun conversation starter.) That day forever changed my relationship with this sport I love so much. I never picked poles up again.

Conformist thinking would have led me to believe I needed ski poles. I refused to accept that as true simply because people said so. Instead, I asked "what if?" As a result, my skiing experience improved dramatically.

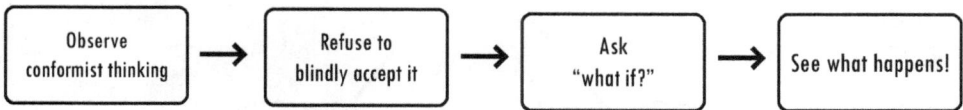

Observe conformist thinking	→	Refuse to blindly accept it	→	Ask "what if?"	→	See what happens!

That simple story provides a vivid example of non-conformist thinking. It demonstrates the beautiful things that can happen when you throw off the shackles of conformity and begin to think independently.

Non-conformity is a hacker superpower. It can be *your* superpower too. Start by asking "what if?" and seeing what happens. The results may surprise you.

How to Apply This to Your Life

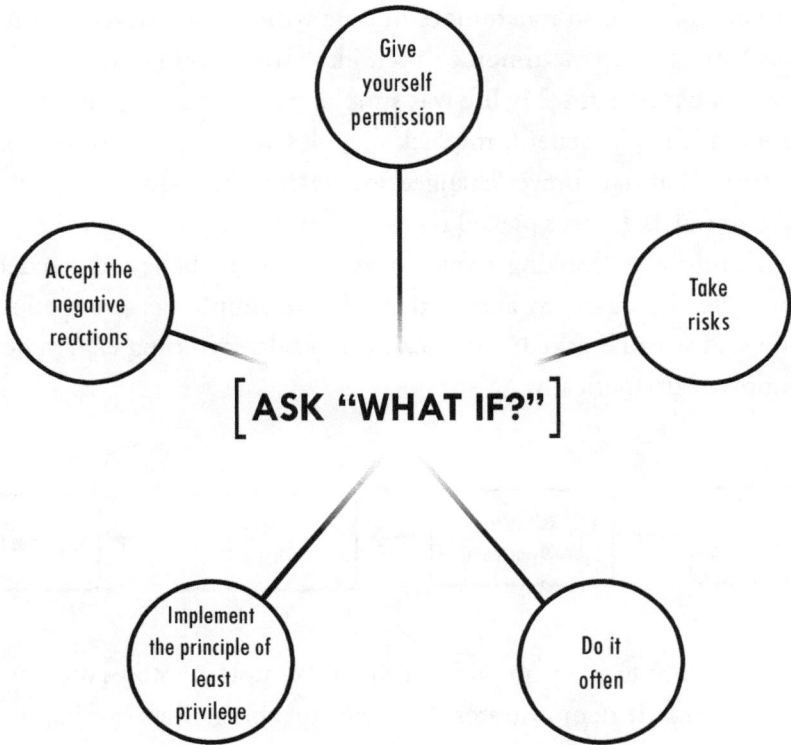

Give yourself permission

Accept the negative reactions

Take risks

$$[\text{ASK "WHAT IF?"}]$$

Implement the principle of least privilege

Do it often

TACTIC #1 Give yourself permission.

Hackers allow themselves to think in extremes. They try unconventional ideas, consider impossible scenarios, and think differently than most people. *They choose to not limit themselves.* That is a *choice.* You can choose to limit yourself, or you can choose to give yourself permission. Either way, you'll choose.

Most people do not give themselves permission. They do not allow themselves to consider ridiculous scenarios, actions, and outcomes. They look to someone else to give them permission to do what they want to do. Hackers give themselves permission to consider *everything*—and to ask "what if" questions. That is a big part of what makes hackers successful.

Most people look at a queue and ask themselves, Where do I get in line? That's the definition of conformity. Hackers look at a queue and ask themselves, Do I actually need to wait in this line? Is there a better way? What if I try to get in through a completely different entrance? What if I skip the line altogether? What if I do something no one's considered? That kind of thinking is the definition of non-conformity.

They simply give themselves permission to think differently.

So give yourself permission. You are the person who is holding you back. Let me repeat that, because it's important: *You are the blocker.* The only thing stopping you is *you*. Recognize that, and consciously choose to get out of your own way. Explore wild concepts. Let go of any constraints you perceive. Don't edit an idea because it seems too expensive, impractical, slow, or ridiculous. Allow yourself the creative freedom to think about *every* idea, because doing so will stretch your thinking.

The power of this tactic scales with the amount of freedom you allow yourself. The more conservative and reserved your thinking is, the less effective the technique will be. The more outrageous and expansive your thoughts, the more transformative the results. So let go of your perceived limitations, give yourself permission to think boldly, and see where you end up.

TACTIC #2 Take risks.

Hackers recognize that non-conformist thinking takes you into uncertain territory. It leads you to question the masses, challenge norms, and believe that you might be right when everyone else is wrong. It's risky. You might face criticism. You might feel like an outsider. You might feel afraid. You might fail.

Do it anyway. Great rewards are often found on the other side of risks.

In the early days of ISE, Steve and I took a risk and deviated from a business norm: We ditched the slide deck. Most companies use polished presentations filled with data, visuals, and talking points when pitching new clients. We wondered, What if we pitched without materials? Would it lead to better more meaningful conversations?

Armed with nothing but notebooks and pens—without laptops or slides—we met with prospective clients. It was risky; those meetings are hard to get. If the experiment failed, we likely wouldn't get another chance. Nevertheless, we believed that if we wanted to help companies build better more secure systems, we'd first need to deeply understand their challenges. It would require listening, not a prepackaged one-size-fits-all pitch.

The experiment worked. I vividly remember walking into a meeting with executives at a major tech company in California. Pretty much the first thing they said to us was, "All right, let's see your pitch."

We could sense their surprise when we responded, "We don't have one. Tell us what you're struggling with."

The executives took a moment to absorb that and then enthusiastically jumped right in. What followed was two hours of open discussion about their goals and roadblocks. At the end of the meeting, the executive in charge turned to us and said, "Thank you for not boring us with slides. This was the best meeting we've had in a long time." That meeting marked the beginning of a lucrative and mutually beneficial partnership that lasted for years.

Taking that risk paid off. It led to a better way of achieving our goals. And much more importantly, it helped our client achieve its goals.

Pursuing an unconventional approach is intimidating. It challenges the familiar and forces you to stand apart from the crowd. But when you take a calculated risk like that, you can uncover shortcuts, challenge assumptions, and discover opportunities others have missed. Every entrepreneur who has disrupted an industry has done exactly that: taken a risk by exploring an unconventional way of doing things.

So measure the risk, take it, and let the question "what if?" guide you to new possibilities.

TACTIC #3 Do it often.

Hackers ask "what if?" every day, about almost everything. They live in a constant state of non-conformity, exploring that question at every opportunity—often without even thinking about it. They apply it to their project work, their daily life, and everything in between.

The best strategy for developing that habit is pretty simple: Just do it a lot. Wherever you are and whatever you're doing, ask "what if?"

What if I did it differently? What if I didn't do it at all? What if I did it ten more times? Or ten fewer times?

Use "what if?" to attack assumptions and explore the opposite of what's expected.

There's a conventional approach to almost everything we do in life, which means there's also an unconventional approach, too (in fact, there are probably endless unconventional approaches). That means there's often an opportunity to ask yourself, What if I tried something different? You don't have to actually implement every unconventional idea you have; the value lies in the thought process. Regularly practicing this exercise will help loosen the mental restraints that are holding you back. The more you ask "what if?" the more natural it will be to deviate from norms, which will lead you to new pathways.

A mentor once taught me a simple technique for getting more keynote opportunities. He said, "If you want to speak more, speak more." His point was that to book more keynotes, I needed to get on more stages—even if the events were inconvenient, required significant travel, or otherwise weren't ideal. He was right. Saying yes to those opportunities enabled me to meet more meeting planners, gain more exposure, and eventually secure the bookings I truly wanted.

The idea here is similar. *If you want to be more unconventional, be unconventional more.* Ask "what if?" regularly, and watch your mindset shift.

TACTIC #4 Implement the principle of least privilege.

In cybersecurity, there are principles regarding the development of systems that make those systems more resistant to attack. They are known as *secure design principles.* They're universal, and they're timeless. One such concept is called the *principle of least privilege*: the idea that users or other entities should be granted only the minimum amount of access or permissions necessary for their tasks. Adhering to the principle reduces the amount of damage that can be done in the event of a security breach.

The principle applies to life as well. We need to limit *who* we allow to influence us, and also limit *how much* we allow those trusted people to influence our thinking.

Consider the idea through the lens of money. Do you take financial advice from just anyone? Hopefully not. If so, please reconsider—because most people are absolutely *terrible* with money. Their advice should be ignored: You don't want to inherit their bad instincts and emotional decision-making. Even among the financially savvy, you still need to be selective. There's no one-size-fits-all financial strategy: Your goals, life stage, and tax situation might be completely different from those of the guru you're listening to.

To counter that, apply the principle of least privilege: Approach situations as though the people or groups involved lack the authority to dictate your actions. (That may sound like it's bordering on anarchy, but stay with me.) Before complying with a request, ask yourself, What if I do? What if I don't? What's the best that could happen? What's the worst that could happen?

Most of the time, you'll find the request is reasonable and following it makes sense. After all, it's being asked of you for a reason. However, that reason probably won't *always* make sense. Sometimes the herd is heading in the wrong direction. Those times are the opportunities you're looking for—moments in which questioning the norm might lead to a better way.

TACTIC #5 Accept the negative reactions.

Ethical hacking isn't always appreciated, even by those it helps. It can make people uncomfortable or trigger other negative reactions. Take security research, for example, in which hackers independently uncover vulnerabilities; companies don't always welcome unsolicited reports pointing out the flaws in their products. Some ignore the findings, while others outright dispute them. In consulting, when hackers are hired to find vulnerabilities, employees close to the project may feel threatened, viewing the hackers' findings as a critique of their competence or a threat to their job security.[26]

---

26 Neither view is correct, by the way. Ethical hackers are there to help build better more secure systems. They are not trying to embarrass anyone or get anyone fired.

When you start asking "what if?" you might encounter resistance too. Accept it and keep going. Non-conformist thinking tends to rattle those who are more comfortable following the herd. Their adverse reactions shouldn't derail you. A negative reaction is not a sign to *stop*—it's usually a sign to *continue*.

The reasons behind these reactions vary: threat to ego, resistance to change, lack of psychological safety, misinterpretation of intent, or emotional attachment to current beliefs. Remember the story about ski poles? The ski instructor became frustrated not because of the questions themselves but because they challenged something he'd spent his entire life teaching. He was forced to consider questions he'd likely never asked himself. That led to an intense, perhaps misplaced sense of frustration. Non-conformity often feels like a threat to those invested in the status quo, and that may cause them to react negatively. Pursue it anyway.

Consider the Salem witch trials, a tragic chapter in Pilgrim-era Massachusetts in which fear, suspicion, and mass hysteria led to the execution of innocent people. Those individuals defied the rigid social, moral, and religious norms of Puritan society, which caused them to be labeled "witches." The accused were generally outliers: independent thinkers, outspoken women, or individuals who didn't conform to other societal expectations.

Simply being different made them a threat to the established order. Being different cost them their lives. Their persecution was driven by fear, prejudice, and groupthink. This dark episode in history highlights the way societies react to those who stand out or think independently. While your own efforts likely won't provoke reactions as extreme, the lesson holds: Society may resist those who dare to think independently. That's okay. Acknowledge that resistance, accept it, and keep moving forward—even when it feels uncomfortable.

QUICK RECAP

- Conformist thinking means accepting things the way they are. Asking "what if?" inspires new ways of thinking.

- Asking "what if" questions frees you from the shackles of conformist thinking and allows you to explore new ways that would otherwise be closed off to you. It is a hacker superpower that will help you think about situations differently.

- Implement the following tactics: give yourself permission, take risks, do it often, implement the principle of least privilege, and accept the negative reactions.

For templates, exercises, and other tools to help you apply this, visit https://tedharrington.com/more.

Asking "what if?" will help you unlock your inner hacker. It will enable you to cultivate a life of non-conformity and find the shortcuts, loopholes, and overlooked assumptions that will help you achieve your goals. Now that you've learned how to apply the mindset to your life, let's recap part II, "Hackers Are Non-Conforming." Then we'll move on to part III, "Hackers Are Committed."

Hackers Are
NON-CONFORMING

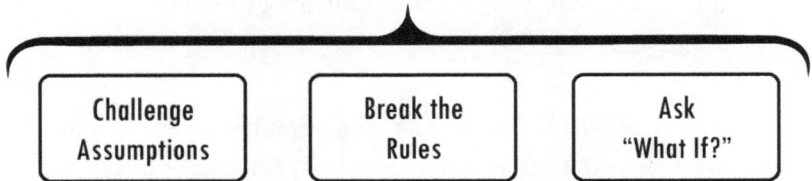

| Challenge Assumptions | Break the Rules | Ask "What If?" |

Hackers are non-conforming. Non-conformity enables hackers to find new and unexpected pathways to achieving their goals. Here's how you can embrace non-conformity too:

Challenge Assumptions

- *Ask other people* as a way to get a fresh perspective on yourself and your own assumptions.

- *Listen to understand* so that you can explore new perspectives and identify and probe your assumptions.

- *Test absolutes* to find the weaknesses in "universal truths" that are in fact not universal.

- *Reflect* to identify lessons about what worked and what didn't.

- *Stress test* your assumptions to find invalid or flawed beliefs; then adjust your approach accordingly.

- *Reject norms* to consciously deviate from the way other people feel required to think.

- *Make it a lifetime practice* so that your thinking won't go stale and will instead continue to evolve.

Break the Rules

- *Understand the purpose of the rule* to identify flaws in its implementation.

- *Evaluate the effectiveness of the rule* to determine whether it is actually delivering the intended result.

- *Determine whether the rule is worth breaking* to ensure that your efforts will bring you closer to your goal (and to avoid wasting energy).

- *Consider the consequences of breaking the rule* so that you can properly weigh the risks.

- *Test the rule (within boundaries)* to explore new pathways without violating moral principles.

- *Advocate for change* to ensure that your rule breaking makes things better.

Ask "What If?"

- *Give yourself permission*, because you are your own biggest blocker.

- *Take risks*, because they will lead you to uncertain places—which is scary, but that's the point of non-conformist thinking.

- *Do it often*, because if you want to be more unconventional, you need to be unconventional more.

- *Implement the principle of least privilege* to reduce the control that outside influences have over you.

- *Accept the negative reactions* to your non-conformist thinking.

PART III

HACKERS ARE COMMITTED

CHAPTER 6

PRIORITIZE PASSION

◆ ◆ ◆

Healthy obsession sustains the effort needed to accomplish big meaningful goals.

Did you know that you can fail kindergarten math?

Let me tell you about Ali. When Ali was in kindergarten, he failed a test on addition and subtraction. The next day, his entire class went on a field trip to the beach—but not Ali. He had to stay behind to take the test again.

Ruthless, these kindergarten teachers.

That experience lit a spark in Ali. Like many people who become hackers, he was inspired by a difficult challenge. He became obsessed with math. Over the years, he steadily improved. By middle school, he was above average. By high school, he was a year ahead of his grade.

It wasn't certain that Ali would go to college; no one in his family ever had. Nevertheless, the pursuit of the unknown inspired Ali. He liked mathematics and wanted to see how far he could take it. He viewed getting into college as a big and worthy challenge. He ultimately achieved that goal and became the first person in his family to go to college.

One fateful day at university, Ali picked up a book on cryptography. That's when everything changed. He'd found his calling.

It turned out that Ali's defining attributes—his passion for math, puzzles, and self-improvement combined with his desire to achieve hard things—also make a skilled cryptographer.

Cryptography is the art of using codes to protect information. It's mathematically intensive, and its purpose is to keep information out of the hands of people who shouldn't have it. It lies at the heart of cybersecurity.

Through his love for cryptography, Ali found the world of ethical hacking. He thrives on finding overlooked assumptions that govern the way a system functions or malfunctions. He's passionate about hacking things that are supposedly "secure" and discovering ways to defeat cryptographic systems. Now Ali is part of the ISE team.

One of the things Ali loves most about hacking is discovering things he's never seen before—not only novel bugs but also unique applications of well-known concepts in unexpected places. He's found countless instances of common web application vulnerabilities like cross-site scripting and cross-site request forgery vulnerabilities.[27] But what really lights him up are the edge cases—the weird, subtle, hard-to-spot issues that no one else has caught. Sometimes they're completely new. Other times, they're rooted in something familiar but hiding in plain sight. For Ali, those discoveries are intellectually stimulating, even thrilling. They feel personal and special because they're not routine. They're uncharted. They're things others have missed.

Recently, a company came to us in crisis: It had just been hacked and had lost more than $10 million in the process. If it happened again, the company would go out of business. It had tried to fix its system but wanted to ensure it was truly secure. So the company hired us, and Ali set out to determine whether the system was still vulnerable.

After some digging, Ali discovered the root cause of the issue: undefined behavior. To understand the concept, consider the rules of the road. In America, you drive on the right; in England, you drive on the left. Your behavior is defined by the country you are in. If the rules were not defined, people would just decide for themselves, and that undefined behavior would result in head-on collisions.

That's essentially what happened to this company. Computer systems enter different states when performing different tasks. System behavior must be defined for each state; otherwise, the system might do something unintended that could allow it to be hacked.

---

27 Cross-site scripting is a security vulnerability that occurs when a site doesn't properly filter untrusted input and allows the injection and execution of harmful code. Cross-site request forgery is a security vulnerability that occurs when a site allows users to execute important actions (like money transfers or password changes) without properly verifying that their requests are legitimate. These flaws are common in web applications and are prime targets for attackers.

That is precisely what happened to this company. Undefined system behavior led to an exploitable security vulnerability.

After the breach, the company tried to fix the issue. However, it misunderstood the problem and focused on the wrong thing. The system wasn't any more secure than before.

Fortunately, we have people like Ali who are obsessed with stuff like this. Thanks to his fanatical interest in the mathematical aspects of computing systems, Ali was able to help the company understand the problem, advise it on fixing the issue, and verify that the remediation worked. The client got a more secure product, and Ali got to have a lot of fun. Today, the company is worth three times what it was worth after getting hacked.

Pretty good outcome for a kid who failed math in kindergarten.

That's the thing about hackers—they succeed because they prioritize passion. They dedicate themselves to the things they love most by constantly improving and accomplishing meaningful goals. Through healthy obsession, they achieve mastery and find fulfillment.

Hackers are willing to invest time, effort, money, and resources in achieving their goals. They're willing to do things that scare them. They're willing to make sacrifices. They're committed, dedicated, and borderline obsessed.

The willingness to do all of that—the sacrifice, the risk, the obsession—starts with prioritizing passion.

That's what you'll want to do too.

Observing This Mindset in the Real World

Want to know what scared the shit out of me?

Writing a book.

Long before *Hackable*, I had a burning desire to write a book. I wanted to contribute something meaningful and lasting. I wanted to help people.

The problem was, though, that writing a book is terrifying. I was scared of being judged, being wrong, or looking like a fool. I was scared that I might write a bad book.

That's the thing about being committed: The things that matter will scare you. They *should* scare you. In fact, if you're not scared, you might not be aiming high enough.

I faced the fear because I was obsessed with the idea. I love big challenges. Maybe I'm a bit of a masochist (I mean, I ran the Boston Marathon for fun), but it's more than that. I like to push myself, test my limits, and see just how big of a boulder I can roll uphill. Above all, I did it because of my passion for helping people. I knew the problem my prospective readers were facing, why it mattered, and how I could help them solve it.[28]

---

28 Tech leaders know they need to secure their systems, but much of the conventional wisdom about how to do so is wrong. I wrote *Hackable* to correct those misconceptions and help companies build more secure systems.

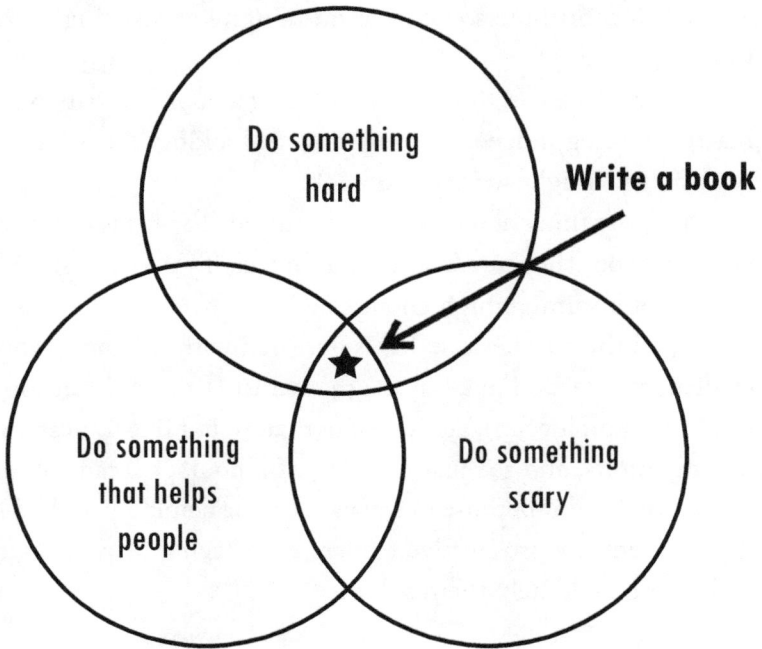

So I set out to write *Hackable*.

For nearly two years, I worked on that book every single day. I was obsessed. I went to bed earlier so that I could wake up earlier. I changed my morning routines so that I could write before dawn, when the day is calmest and my brain is clearest. I wrote over the weekend. I wrote on vacation. I even *took* vacation to write.

I was absolutely, utterly obsessed.

I remember one Saturday in particular. It started like any other: up at 4:30 a.m., coffee, writing by 5:00 a.m.

A little while later, a thought flickered into my awareness. *Am I supposed to meet friends for brunch today?*

"Oh yeah," I muttered to myself. "Brunch at 10. Should probably get ready soon."

I looked at my watch and was shocked to see that it was already well past 2:00 p.m. I'd been so immersed in the project that I'd completely lost track of time. I'd been hammering away at the keyboard for *nine hours*. On a Saturday! I was still in my pajamas, a disheveled mess, while my friends had already exercised, brunched, and moved on with their day.

That's passion. When you chase what you love, time melts away. You prioritize it above everything else.[29]

Hackable took me seventeen months to write—plus the ten years I spent acquiring the insights it contains before I started writing. It required me to wake up ridiculously early, add hours to already busy days, and sacrifice time with friends and family. I poured over 3,000 hours into it.

It was hard, but it was worth it.

When *Hackable* was published, my life changed. Even though I felt like the same person, the world around me began to shift. I started getting better keynote opportunities. I found myself on massive beautifully produced stages in front of thousands of people. Our security companies attracted new clients. But the best part— *by far*—was hearing from people the book had helped. After keynotes, at hacker conventions, and online, strangers approached me to share how the book had reshaped their thinking, improved their security programs, or helped them solve real problems.

Becoming an author has been wildly fulfilling.

That's why passion is crucial. It fuels commitment. It helps you achieve big meaningful goals that require time, effort, money, and

---

29 I don't recommend sacrificing your social life. That's the fast track to misery and loneliness, no matter what the "grind" influencers might say. Nevertheless, it sometimes happens when you pursue something you're truly passionate about.

resources. It keeps you moving forward when you're scared, facing setbacks, or finding a task to be harder than expected. When you prioritize passion, you almost can't fail.

So be passionate. Be positively obsessed. Chase the brass ring simply for the sake of getting it. Leverage that desire to achieve change that is meaningful to you.

That's what hackers do. You can too.

How to Apply This to Your Life

At first, I struggled to write about this concept. *Passion* felt squishy, vague, and frustratingly unactionable. You don't need some indulgent, clichéd social media "inspiration" bullshit. You need something actionable and realistic.

To make the advice in this chapter useful, I relied on the same strategy I used for everything else in this book: I looked at what hackers do. They're the definition of passionate. By studying their behavior, I identified some tangible actions you can emulate.

The advice to prioritize passion is both good and bad. In theory, it's simple: Do what makes you feel alive. In practice, however, two challenges get in the way.

First, most people don't know themselves well enough to identify their passions. Ideally, passion should be obvious. If you're excited about something, pursue it. If not, don't. But it's rarely that simple. It takes real introspection to recognize what you're truly drawn to.

Second, even if you've identified your passion, you might wonder what to *do* with that passion—especially if it doesn't align with your job or help pay the bills. That's okay. Prioritizing passion doesn't mean monetizing it right away. It just means making space for your passion—at work or after hours on your own dime. Eventually, it'll lead to exciting new opportunities.

Many hackers have overcome both problems. They've identified what excites them, and they've found time for it. Try the following tactics, and see whether they help you do the same.

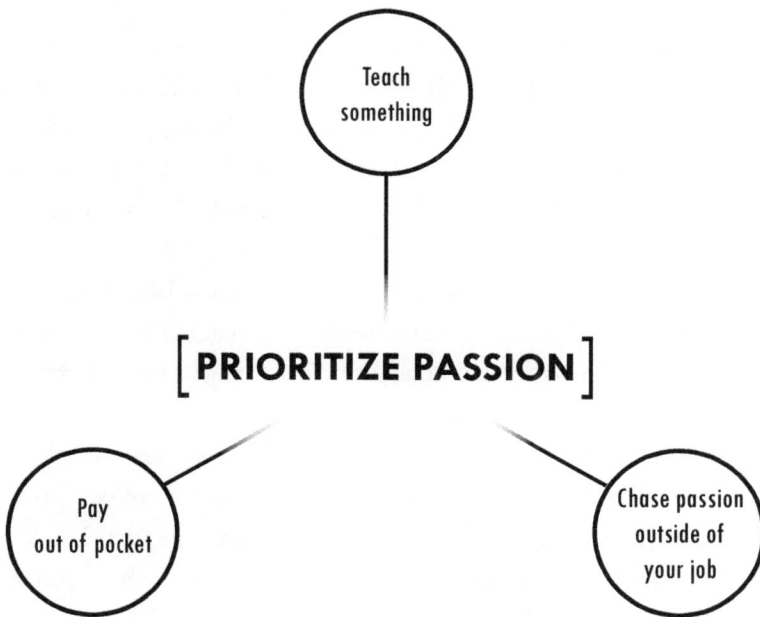

```
                    ╭─────────╮
                    │  Teach  │
                    │something│
                    ╰────┬────╯
                         │
                         │
      [ PRIORITIZE PASSION ]
       ╱                        ╲
  ╭─────────╮              ╭──────────╮
  │   Pay   │              │Chase passion│
  │out of pocket│          │ outside of │
  ╰─────────╯              │  your job  │
                           ╰──────────╯
```

TACTIC #1 **Teach something.**

A mentor once taught me that the best way to learn is to teach. Teaching a concept to others forces you to understand it more deeply. It can also be illuminating: When you find something that you enjoy teaching others, you find something you're passionate about.

Hackers love to hack, and they also love to teach. I've seen that passion for teaching firsthand at ISE, and it's remarkable: Almost everywhere I look—both online and in person—I find our hackers sharing their knowledge with others. Walking through the office, I regularly see people huddled together around someone who is demonstrating a new technique or a better way to use a tool. Our internal messaging app constantly lights up with messages sharing articles, videos, books, courses, and other resources people are learning from.

Another way I've seen hackers teach is through a cool concept we implemented at ISE called *fire talks*. Basically, anyone at the company can volunteer to teach an idea to whoever would like to learn it during lunch. The talks are informal, often impromptu; some prepare a bit or make slides, while others don't. The talks cover everything from highly technical exploit sequences to research findings to productivity tips and other life hacks. One recent talk was about how to make homemade butter! Teaching and learning are inseparable ideas for hackers: They know that to get better, you have to consistently do both.

As you work to prioritize your passion, focus on teaching something to someone else. You don't need to become a college professor; just share an idea with a boss, peer, or direct report. Look for opportunities to teach, and tune in to how you feel while doing it. If you feel a spark—if you are energized and excited about what you're teaching—you've likely found a passion worth pursuing. If you find teaching a subject tedious and boring, keep looking—it's not your passion.

Teaching is a powerful way to uncover what drives you while learning *and* helping other people. That's a win on three fronts!

Start teaching and see what it reveals.

TACTIC #2 Chase passion outside of your job.

Ethical hacking is now a well-established profession, but it wasn't always that way. Early hackers couldn't pursue their passion as their day job—back then, the roles didn't exist because the profession didn't exist. They *had* to pursue their passion outside of their normal jobs. Even today, many hackers hold unrelated jobs. Some work in other security disciplines, while others don't work in security at all. Whatever the circumstances, they love to hack, so they find ways to do it on their own time. They hack in the evening, over the weekend, and while on vacation.

You can find time for your passion too. Identify aspects of your goals that can be pursued as side hustles, hobbies, or extracurricular activities. That way, you'll be able to work on what you're truly passionate about, free from the constraints of your day job. Outside of work, you can specialize, focus, and find joy. The skills and experience you gain will prepare you to seize new opportunities when they arise.

This advice isn't just for early- or mid-career professionals. Even senior leaders need to put in extra effort to level up into the lofty positions above them. Those jobs are scarce, lucrative, and in demand. To win out against fierce competition, you'll need every advantage you can get. You can obtain those advantages outside of your current job.

TACTIC #3 Pay out of pocket.

The biggest annual hacker convention is called DEF CON, and it's awesome. It's an opportunity to hear about groundbreaking research, participate in hands-on labs, compete in hacking contests, and connect with new and old friends alike.

There's a strong business case for companies to send their security staff to DEF CON—yet far fewer do than you'd expect. Furthermore, for hackers who don't hold security jobs, obtaining employer funding for a trip to DEF CON is unlikely. However, that fact doesn't deter hackers from going; in fact, many attendees spend their own money to get there. I can't think of any other professional conferences where I've met anyone who paid their own way to attend. Do people spend their own money to attend insurance conferences, for instance? Maybe. It's certainly uncommon, though.

Hackers are so motivated to improve their hacking skills that they'll fund their trips to hacker conventions themselves if their employers won't. That illustrates the power of passion: If you care about something, you're willing to sacrifice time and money for it.[30]

Not every investment requires money, though; there are tons of free resources for learning about almost anything one could want to explore. Online hacking labs, for example, provide real-world environments for practicing hands-on skills. There are free cybersecurity courses that cover topics like penetration testing, social engineering, and network defense. By keeping up with blogs, podcasts, and online communities, hackers can benefit from near-constant exposure to new techniques and emerging threats—all for free. But even free resources do have a cost: time. The investment might not be a financial one, but it's still real. Hackers know that skill building is a commitment, whether it costs dollars or hours.

The people who make the most progress are often the ones who invest their own money in themselves. They buy the book.

---

30 This is a tricky topic to discuss because self-funding a trip to a conference simply isn't an option for many people. As in any community, there are people in the hacker community who are unemployed, underemployed, still completing their studies, or struggling with significant debts and obligations. For many, there is no discretionary money for things like attending conferences. For others, traveling to a conference is simply impractical, especially if it's in another country. I have empathy for those people, and I don't mean to add stress to an already difficult dynamic. The point, however, remains true: Many people who attend hacker conventions pay their own way to get there.

They take the paid course. They pay to attend the conference their company wouldn't cover.

The same principle applies outside of hacking: The most dedicated people actively invest in their own development. Entrepreneurs can take business courses or join online communities to learn from others who've built successful companies. Creatives can study problem-solving, mental models, and storytelling through structured classes or informal tutorials. Anyone can develop negotiation, decision-making, and influencing skills by exploring educational blogs, podcasts, or university content. Even if you're starting from scratch—whether it's coding, public speaking, or critical thinking—there are high-quality resources out there to help you grow. Some cost money; others just take time.

As you think about your own goals, look for opportunities to personally invest in them. Many people are unwilling to do anything educational unless it is funded by their employer; while those people are not wrong to feel that way, it definitely does not help them advance their big goals. Don't fall into that trap. Instead, act like a hacker. Invest in your passions.

Extraordinarily successful people often say that even when they were at their poorest, they did not limit their spending on education, training, or professional development. The investments you make in yourself and your passion will eventually pay off.

QUICK RECAP

► Healthy obsession sustains the effort needed to accomplish big meaningful goals.

► Identifying your passions can be challenging. Practice introspection to better understand yourself and uncover passions you might not have been aware of.

► Implement the following tactics: teach something, chase passion outside of your job, and pay out of pocket.

For templates, exercises, and other tools to help you apply this, visit https://tedharrington.com/more.

Now that you've learned why and how to prioritize passion, you may be wondering whether that's truly always possible. What about when things get difficult? Let's answer that question by digging into the idea of tenacity.

CHAPTER 7

PERSIST

◆ ◆ ◆

Tenacity enables you to overcome long odds, insurmountable obstacles, and deflating setbacks.

My friend Natalie is a talented hacker. She works for the internal security team at a large tech company, where she recently ran into a frustrating but common problem: People wouldn't listen to her.

Let me explain with an analogy. The goal of auto racing is to reach the finish line as fast as possible. But while speed wins, speed also kills. The key is control. That's where brakes come in.

The faster you're going and the sharper the turns, the more important brakes become. The paradox is that brakes don't slow you down—they help you go *faster*. Without them, every car would crash on the first turn. Races are won on the turns, not the straightaways.

The same is true in business. The security team is the brakes. It doesn't exist to stop momentum—it exists to navigate risk and set the business up for maximum velocity. Used correctly, the security team helps the business take smarter risks and move faster.

Unfortunately, many companies don't see it that way.

Many don't want to factor security into their business decisions. Some outright ignore blatant security concerns. That's like trying to win a race without brakes. You'll not only certainly lose but also likely explode into a wall, too.

Why do businesses operate that way?

First and foremost, it's due to a misguided focus on urgency. When businesses make decisions, they want to enact them immediately. The smart move would be to first evaluate the potential risk to security, but unfortunately, that move is often perceived as slowing things down. Urgency overpowers prudence.[31]

Second, security is hard to understand. Executives are responsible for many domains, and security is just one of them. However, many executives view security not as its own domain but rather as a subset of another one (such as technology). Few executives come up through the ranks in security roles, so they don't have hands-on experience with it. There is little formal education on security, and basically none of it caters to executives. If executives don't fully

---

31 This is such a big problem that I wrote an entire section about it in
    Hackable titled "No, Security Does Not Slow You Down."

understand security, it can be difficult for them to see a reason to invest in it.

Third, businesses themselves do not incentivize security. They tend to reward other things, especially performance on revenue and profit. Those incentives drive behavior that is usually not aligned with security.

For those reasons, security professionals struggle when raising concerns about security to their leadership. Overcoming these hurdles requires tenacity. A *lot* of it. My friend Natalie's story is a perfect example of that.

Her company was planning to launch a product that leveraged a new technology. The product would offer her company a new way to make money, engage customers, improve efficiency, and generate press coverage, all of which should result in massive profits.

Should.

If the tech was hacked, it would torpedo sales and scare away customers. It would definitely generate press coverage—just not the kind the company was hoping for.

What concerned Natalie was that the tech provided access to the company's most valuable digital assets but hadn't been through rigorous security testing. If hacked, this system would expose intellectual property, sensitive data, and personal information. And, as is the case for any new system, the ways to attack it weren't yet understood. That combination—high-value assets, new tech, and a lack of testing—is a dangerous mix. Attackers *love* that combination. It's juicy, it's easy to exploit, and it delivers big returns.

Natalie cautioned the company's executives to have the product tested for security vulnerabilities prior to its rollout. The executives were not interested in that. Her warnings were ignored.

Nevertheless, Natalie kept insisting. She highlighted company policy requiring any new tech that touched sensitive digital assets

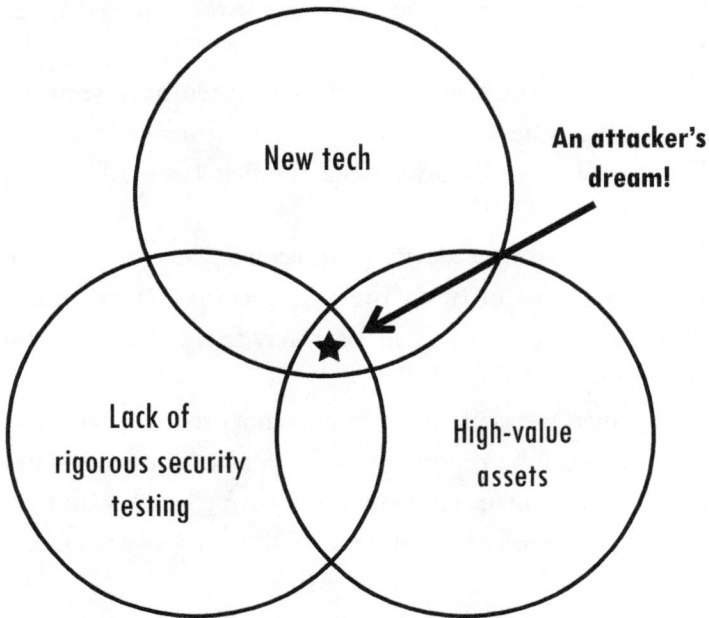

to go through a security review. The executives acknowledged the policy but noted that the product's cloud infrastructure had already been through a security assessment, so the larger product must be fine. That is a common but heavily flawed assumption.[32] Nevertheless, the assumption prevailed. The product team assumed they'd already done enough and dismissed the warnings about security.

Undeterred, Natalie opted to inspect the system herself. She figured that if she could discover its security flaws, the execs might

---

32   Securing the cloud infrastructure of an application is not the same as securing the application itself. Cloud infrastructure is like the foundation of a house. It can be as secure as you'd like, but that doesn't mean that the house you build on top of it will keep thieves out. That part needs to be considered too.

pause to consider their implications. The product launched without undergoing a security assessment, and Natalie got to work. Although it meant going above and beyond her official responsibilities on that project, she knew it was important. So she conducted a professional, responsible assessment of the system—and almost immediately, she found a critical security vulnerability: the return of verbose error messages that exposed the product's entire SQL database. The issue meant that attackers—without any privileges at all—could access sensitive data. They could steal it, sell it, change it, destroy it, or hold it hostage. Any of those actions would result in significant financial damage to the company. The worst damage would be to its reputation. This company is known all over the world, and its brand is its most valuable asset. Launching a product that violated the trust of its customer base would have been horrible for the business.

Upon finding that critical security vulnerability, Natalie went through the proper channels to report it, including to the responsible executives as well as the legal department. Word spread quickly, making its way to the desk of the CEO. Like a race car driver, he wanted to approach the dangerous curve aggressively, but with control. With the catastrophic vulnerability known, the higher-ups reached a consensus on what to do next: engage a security consulting firm. That's when ISE got involved. What followed was a security assessment that took a couple of months and found dozens more security issues just like the one Natalie had found. That's the beauty of security testing: Once the enterprise knew about the product's problems, the team could fix them. After a short period, the ongoing rollout of the product was back on track—then with a much more *secure* product.

It was all thanks to tenacity.

Natalie would not rest no matter how many obstacles she hit. That's what hackers do—they relentlessly pursue their objectives.

They are motivated even in the face of continual setbacks, resistance, objections, and rejections. Hackers do not quit easily.

I was in Finland recently and learned about a concept known as *sisu*. It doesn't have a direct translation in English, but it can be understood as "extraordinary determination and courage in the face of extreme adversity." Sisu is about strength of will. It is not about momentary courage but rather the ability to sustain that courage over time. Sisu is the spirit of a person who forges ahead despite impossibly long odds, has hope even in the bleakest scenarios, and refuses to quit.

That's what we are talking about here.

Success is a lagging indicator. First comes effort; *then* comes success. You cannot skip the first part. Hackers don't just click a single button and find an exploitable vulnerability; they work at it over time until eventually, they find one. Successful people put in the work first. There is no such thing as an "overnight success." Even people who seem like they magically appeared in a position of prominence did not arrive there by chance—they worked hard to get there.

There is only one way.

That way is *tenacity*.

Observing This Mindset in the Real World

For most of my life, I wanted to give a TED Talk. Doing so could help people. It could inspire change. It would also be *extremely* hard. Needless to say, I wanted it. *Badly*.

In case you aren't familiar with them, TED Talks are short presentations about ideas with the potential to change the world.[33] They're delivered by experts on beautifully produced stages, and

33 https://www.ted.com/.

their messages reach a massive worldwide audience.

The problem was that many years ago, at the start of my cybersecurity career, I wasn't much of an authority on anything. I'd also never given a talk—certainly not one at that scale—so the idea of delivering a TED Talk felt impossibly out of reach.

Still, I knew how to break a big goal into smaller steps. I realized I needed to do three things: gain useful insights, build authority, and develop speaking skills. So I decided to give a talk at a local conference. In hindsight, even that was a bold move. I didn't have deep expertise in hacking yet, and I'd never spoken in front of an audience. Yet there I was, planning to teach a room full of people about hacking without having experience to back me up.

Like I said, bold.

That's the thing about being tenacious—you're willing to overcome no matter what. So I applied for speaking opportunities even though I was unqualified.

That's when I ran into the next barrier: I simply wasn't credible.

Conferences want to hear from experts, not novices like I was at the time. Being new to hacking didn't exactly inspire confidence that I'd deliver value to the audience.

To solve that problem, I borrowed ISE's credentials. I'd be presenting ideas from our security research, so I let that research serve as my credibility. It took a while, but eventually, I convinced a conference to take a risk on me. Shortly thereafter, I found myself alone on a stage, shivering from terror under the bright lights and wondering what the hell I was doing.

That first talk was...not terrible. It was not good, by any measure—but it was not a complete mess, either. In preparing for the talk, I'd had intense bouts of imposter syndrome. I'd worried I would fail, be wrong, and embarrass myself. Fortunately, none of those fears came true.

Preparing for that talk required me to interview our ethical hackers. I organized the insights I gleaned from those conversations into something actionable. I shaped stories and figured out how to share data visually. Then I rehearsed my butt off so that I wouldn't embarrass myself.

I'm so glad I did it.

The talk went okay, and I even met a prospective new customer. I knew I was onto something, so I went all out. Over the following years, I built a system for pursuing and delivering talks. Seven years later, I had scaled my talk output to roughly fifty talks per year. *Fifty!*

At the same time, we had systematically grown our ethical hacking company. We had solidified our authority by publishing research that was covered in outlets such as *The New York Times*, *The Washington Post*, *USA Today*, and *Forbes*. We had expanded our customer base, adding companies ranging from hot new start-ups to titans of tech.

After nearly a decade of leading security teams and shaping conversations about hacking, I was ready. It was time to get on a TED stage. As it turned out, TED wasn't ready for me. Or more precisely, TED didn't think I was ready for *them*.

I had already been considered for a TED Talk several times. Cybersecurity had become a hot topic, I had insights backed by research, and I'd developed some degree of speaking ability. However, I kept getting rejected in the end.

I was frustrated. I knew I could help people. I had the insight, the skills, and the drive. But it still wasn't enough. As I pondered my position, I came to a realization:

1. I had not established *my* authority. I needed to demonstrate it in a different way.

2. I had not sharpened an idea worthy of a TED Talk. I needed
to better hone my ideas.

With that realization, the solution became clear: I needed to
write a book.

What followed was my journey to writing *Hackable*, which you
read a little bit about in the last chapter. That experience changed
my life in so many magical ways, in particular by moving me closer
to this massive and exciting goal of delivering a TED Talk.

I spent a couple of years writing and then launching *Hackable*.
After that, I returned my focus to getting myself a TED Talk.

And let me tell you, things were different.

Before becoming an author, I'd been a TED Talk finalist several
times over many years. I'd been rejected each time. Then, a mere
month after becoming an author, I was selected for *two* different
TED Talks.

That's *wild*.

As I found myself in the bewildering situation of *declining a
TED Talk* (because you can do only one per year), I paused to reflect
on how far I'd come.

It had taken me more than ten years. I'd started with no authority, no credibility, and no speaking skills. I'd met a number of massive roadblocks along the way. But I kept going. I systematically
tackled each obstacle as it presented itself. Eventually, I achieved
my goal by delivering a talk titled "Why You Need to Think Like a
Hacker" at TEDxFrankfurt. That talk became this book.[34]

That's the power of tenacity. When you are tenacious, you

---

34 I think this is where I'm supposed to make a shameless plug, suggesting that
you invite me to be the keynote speaker at your next event.

persist and persevere. You do whatever it takes to overcome long odds, insurmountable obstacles, and deflating setbacks.

That's exactly how hackers approach things.

Hackers are relentless. They go over, under, around, or through the many obstacles that present themselves. Hackers persist.

Hackers are committed.

You should be too.[35]

---

35 Do you want to give a TED Talk someday? I wrote a step-by-step guide outlining how I did it in case you want to as well. Find it at https://tedharrington.com/more.

How to Apply This to Your Life

Tenacity is an attitude. Here are some ways to implement it in your own life.

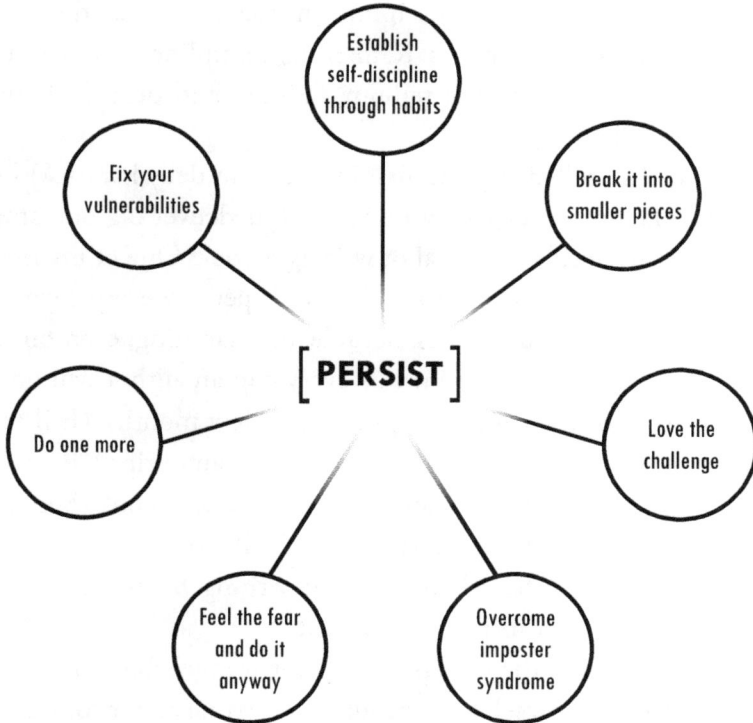

Establish self-discipline through habits

Fix your vulnerabilities

Break it into smaller pieces

[PERSIST]

Do one more

Love the challenge

Feel the fear and do it anyway

Overcome imposter syndrome

TACTIC #1 **Establish self-discipline through habits.**

Hackers don't quit easily, and it is through their relentless effort that they eventually find security vulnerabilities that everyone else has missed. Hackers also *want* to hack all the time, so if it's not their day job, they make time for it and build habits that will support it.

People often think that big goals require motivation or inspiration. That's incorrect. Inspiration only gets you *started*—it quickly wanes, and it doesn't help you *finish*. Big goals require sustained effort, and sustained effort is about *discipline*, not inspiration. Self-discipline is the practice of managing your behaviors to achieve a specific goal. Discipline enables you to handle resistance, obstacles, and setbacks. Remaining disciplined is one of the ways hackers overcome the tedium, failures, and dead ends that hacking entails.

To establish self-discipline, first inspect your daily habits. When properly practiced over a long period, habits deliver big outcomes. For example, consider the goal of writing a book. One of my mentors encourages authors to write 250 words per day every day until the book is done. That feels achievable, not daunting, even on the worst days. At a pace of 250 words every day, an author will finish the first draft of their manuscript in just a few months. (It'll take years to edit it, but at least they'll have a manuscript!) Pause to think about that: Tons of people want to write a book. Some of them start, yet few of them actually finish. The ones who *do* finish are the ones who established a regular writing habit rather than giving up when their inspiration ran out.

There's a simple three-step process for using habits to achieve your goals. I use it myself and encourage everyone at our companies to use it too.

First, define the end goal. Just capture the vibe of the goal, even if it's abstract and hard to measure. Something like "Expand my professional network" would do it.

Second, define the measurement you'll use to judge your success. What data point will determine—objectively—whether you've achieved the goal? For the previous example, the measurement might be something like "Held 100 in-person meetings to strengthen relationships with key industry contacts, including customers, prospects, and influential figures."

Third, define the habits you'll need to arrive at that metric. In the case of our example, it might be something like "One day a week, I'll spend three hours coordinating meetings, and I'll block off two days a week to have the meetings."

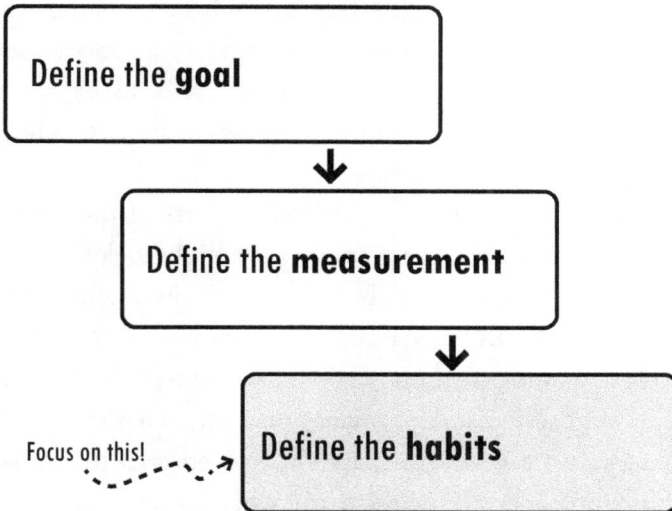

Once you've done all three steps, you can focus solely on actually building those habits. Habits can be controlled; outcomes cannot. Detailed guidance on building habits is beyond the scope of this book, but you can learn from the best by reading *Atomic Habits* by James Clear and *Make Time* by Jake Knapp and John Zeratsky.[36]

---

36 https://jamesclear.com/atomic-habits; https://maketime.blog/.

The former will teach you how to build habits, and the latter will teach you how to carve out time for those new habits.

Developing self-discipline and habits (as well as the necessary time management skills) will enable you to sustain the long-term effort required to achieve your big goals.

`TACTIC #2` Break it into smaller pieces.

Most exploits require many steps. You don't hack a system in one click. So what do hackers do? They study how the system works, identify how to access valuable assets, find flaws in the way the system protects those assets, and devise ways to exploit those flaws. They break the process into manageable steps, tackling each one in sequence.

They begin by exploring the individual parts of the system and how each of them works. For example, they might look at a shopping website not as a single system but as a collection of smaller parts: a login page that checks the validity of username/password combos, a registration page for creating new user accounts, a product catalog, and a checkout system and payment processor, to name a few.

By analyzing each part separately, hackers can test how each piece functions, identify whether (or where) each piece fails, and look for ways to trigger unexpected interactions that could make the system do something it shouldn't. A powerful way to take a system that is supposed to do X and see whether it can instead do Y is to study how the individual parts work—and fail—on their own.

That's how you'll want to think too. There's a famous proverb that asks, *"What's the best way to eat an elephant?"* One bite at a time. That's the idea here: Big complex goals cannot be achieved in one motion just as you can't eat an elephant in one bite. However, small bites taken one at a time will eventually get you there. Break your goal down into its discrete components; then tackle them one by one.

The previous tactic gave you an exercise that will help you translate your goals into daily habits. But sometimes, even if you have good habits in place, a goal can still feel overwhelming. This tactic will teach you how to make big goals less intimidating by splitting them into milestones and then tackling those milestones step by step. There's a simple exercise for that.

First, define the goal. Write down your desired outcome in clear, specific terms, such as "Land a senior leadership role with at least 50 people in my reporting structure."

Second, outline the milestones. Identify the primary interim achievements required to reach the end goal, and put them in order. In the leadership role example, the milestones might be the following:

1. Position yourself for roles at the right level (such as director, VP, or head of a certain department or team)

2. Gain experience managing teams amid layers of leadership

3. Build relationships with executive-level hiring influencers

For each milestone, identify three key elements:

1. **Success criteria:** How will you know when you've reached the milestone? To continue the example above, the criteria might include being shortlisted for three VP-level roles in a certain quarter, getting a final interview, or being offered a job.

2. **Requirements:** What resources, skills, or support will you need? You might need a polished executive résumé, strategic leadership experience, or strong internal sponsorship, for example.

3. **Constraints:** What obstacles might you face? Perhaps you'll need to overcome visibility gaps, internal competition, or a lack of prior experience in managing a larger team.

Third, list the specific actions required to achieve your goal. Once you've done that, it's time to execute those actions. In our example, that could mean updating your LinkedIn profile and résumé to reflect strategic *leadership achievements*, not just *years of experience*. It could mean asking a trusted mentor to help you refine your executive narrative. It could also mean applying for stretch roles, even outside of your current company or industry.

Once you've reached a milestone, move on to the next one. Develop a plan for addressing constraints and satisfying each requirement. Focus only on the current milestone until it is complete. Then move on to the next one.

In electrical engineering, circuits are designed in either parallel or series configurations. Parallel circuits allow multiple components to operate independently because each has its own direct path to the power source. For example, the lights in your home are wired in parallel so that turning one off doesn't affect the others. By contrast, series circuits connect components sequentially such that a current flows through one component to the next. A string of old holiday lights is a classic example. If one bulb burns out, the whole string stops working. Every bulb needs to be powered in order, with no exceptions. One by one, the whole strand is lit.

You'll want to approach your goal as though it's a series circuit: one "bulb" at a time. Just as power flows to the first bulb and then to the second, complete each milestone before moving on to the next. Your big goals will feel more achievable as you break them into smaller more manageable pieces.

Tenacity is not one long race; it's a bunch of short races, one after another, all heading in the same direction.

`TACTIC #3` Love the challenge.

Hackers view difficulty differently than most people. While most people prefer things to be easy, hackers are the opposite. Steve once told me that he was drawn to hacking because for him, "it's all about the challenge." If something is considered hard to achieve, it becomes interesting. If it's labeled "impossible," it becomes irresistible. Hackers find joy in their work not *despite* the difficulty, but *because* of it.

That's a mindset you'll want to adopt too. The most fulfilling achievements require time and effort, trigger fear, are filled with friction, and come riddled with setbacks. All too often, we limit our potential by setting goals that allow us to avoid challenges. They are too easy, too soft, and too small. When you think like a hacker, you set ambitious goals and embrace the challenges that come with them.

Whatever your goal, difficulty is inevitable. The key is in how you perceive it. Do you see a challenge as an annoyance to remove or a barrier to smash through? Is it frustrating or exciting? The hacker way is to fall in love with the challenge. Do it *because* it is hard. Find joy in difficulty. Convert setbacks into opportunities to develop your skills and grow. Treat every challenge as a puzzle to solve.

This simple shift in thinking will support the tenacity that big goals require. Rather than avoiding the struggle, you'll begin to relish it.

There is a mantra I've learned from members of the military: "Embrace the suck." Born from the relentless challenges of military life, the phrase encourages the acceptance of present discomfort as a requirement for achieving something greater. When you chase big worthy goals and face resistance, rejections, or setbacks, it sucks. It feels uncomfortable, frustrating, and exhausting. But leaning in to that discomfort strengthens you. It tempers your resolve, enables you to build camaraderie with the people you're in the trenches with, and makes the victory sweeter. It gives you a chance to test your mettle and discover what you're truly made of.

Without struggle, we'd never get to level up our skills. We'd never get to be tenacious or experience the feeling of overcoming our obstacles. When difficulties arise, don't get frustrated. Relish the challenge.

TACTIC #4 Overcome imposter syndrome.

Tenacity requires us to push through fear, and one of the most common fears that holds people back is imposter syndrome. Imposter syndrome is a psychological phenomenon that causes individuals to doubt their skills or talents even when they are highly competent.

Ironically, imposter syndrome tends to afflict those who are already skilled or close to mastering their craft. Many of the brilliant hackers I work with often doubt themselves, believing they're unqualified to give a talk, write a paper, or appear on the news. Despite being more knowledgeable than most, they focus on the few things they *don't* know rather than the vast expertise they do have.

If left unchecked, imposter syndrome can prevent you from achieving meaningful goals. If you believe you're not qualified, you might not try at all. If you don't try, you can't succeed. To overcome imposter syndrome, take the following steps.

First, acknowledge your feeling of inadequacy. Ignoring the feeling won't make it go away. Name the emotion behind the feeling, whether it's fear, doubt, anxiety, or something else. That will separate you from the feeling and help you recognize it as just that: a feeling, not a fact.

Second, reframe it as a positive. Imposter syndrome is actually a good thing. It means that you have a growth mindset. It indicates that you're aware of areas for improvement and strive to be better. Instead of focusing on what you lack and allowing it to hold you back, recognize imposter syndrome as a sign of your ambition and dedication to growth.

Third, focus on helping others. For example, if you are scared to give a talk, don't focus on your own insecurity; focus on someone who desperately needs your knowledge. Your talk will help that person grow. Helping that person is a kindness and an act of service.

Fourth, focus on the cheers, not the boos. If you experience imposter syndrome, you tend to think that everyone is going to hate whatever you share (and, by extension, hate you for sharing it). Unfortunately, that assumption is often reinforced by the "trolls" who make the internet a terrible place. However, most people root for other people. How do *you* think about others? Do you hope to see them fail or hope to learn from them? I'm guessing it's the latter. Most people are kind. Focus on them, not on the vocal minority spewing unfair criticism. Their ugly spirit is a reflection on themselves, not on you.

Those strategies will help you bypass imposter syndrome, one of the biggest internal barriers to achieving your goals. The willingness to confront and overcome such barriers lies at the very heart of tenacity.

[**Overcoming Imposter Syndrome**]

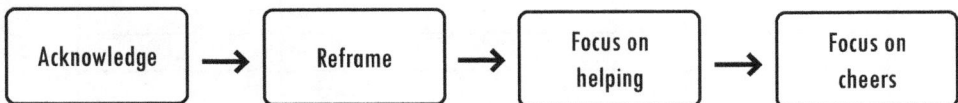

| Acknowledge | → | Reframe | → | Focus on helping | → | Focus on cheers |

`TACTIC #5` **Feel the fear and do it anyway.**

Imposter syndrome isn't the only fear that hackers face. Like anyone else, they might fear failing, being misunderstood, or becoming obsolete. Hackers also encounter unique fears: legal ambiguity, misuse of their work, reputational damage, or a loss of anonymity. Yet fear itself—not the actual outcomes that we worry about—is often the biggest threat to our success. As Franklin D. Roosevelt famously said, "The only thing we have to fear is fear itself." Few fears actually come true, but if you don't try at all, failure is guaranteed.

The year that I spoke at TEDxFrankfurt, the event's theme was "feel the fear and do it anyway." It resonated so strongly with me that I commissioned a Los Angeles street artist to graffiti the slogan for me. It now hangs in my office as a daily reminder to be tenacious even when I'm scared.

We've already discussed ways to overcome imposter syndrome, but what about tackling other fears? One powerful method is what I call *fear canceling*. This exercise breaks fears down into manageable parts, helping you see them for what they are so that you can "cancel" them. The publisher of *Hackable* taught me this exercise, and I used it to address the many profound fears I had about being a first-time author. Here's how it works.

First, draw four columns.

In the first column, write down your fear. I named my fear plainly.

Fear	Impact	Likelihood	Mitigation

I was afraid I might write a bad book. I was afraid that despite all the time and effort I'd invested in it, I'd end up with a crappy book.

In the next column, describe what would happen if the fear came true. For me, writing a bad book could have been embarrassing at best and could have undermined my professional credibility at worst.

In the third column, estimate how *likely* the fear is to come true. This part is subjective but still valuable. You can use relative terms like "unlikely" or numerical estimates like "10%." I wrote "medium."

In the final column, write down actions that could reduce or eliminate the likelihood of the fear coming true. For my example, the remedy to my fear of writing a bad book was simple: *Write a good book.*

That moment changed everything for me. I literally felt the tension ease from my shoulders—tension I hadn't even realized I was carrying. I relaxed, because now I knew what I had to do. That clarity was freeing.

Breaking the fear down transformed it completely. What had been a vague, overwhelming dread became something tangible and actionable. I didn't yet know how to write a good book, but at least I had a path forward: I'd define what makes a book "good," then make sure mine met the criteria. That gave me direction. More importantly, it removed the fear's power over me.

Fear is the number one reason people who start writing a book don't finish. This exercise ensured I wasn't one of them. I'll leave it to the readers of *Hackable* to decide whether I wrote a good book—but I'm confident I at least didn't write a bad one.

Before I tried "fear canceling," the fear was abstract and overwhelming. After, it was concrete and manageable. I knew what to do.

Repeat this exercise for every fear related to your goal. By the time you've worked through them all, you'll have cleared away some of the biggest mental obstacles standing in your way.

TACTIC #6 Do one more.

Hackers succeed because they refuse to give up. Hacking is difficult; it's riddled with roadblocks and setbacks. You try one technique—nothing. Another—still nothing. A third—same result. Nevertheless, *you keep trying*.

There is a direct correlation between the effort devoted to a security assessment and the number of vulnerabilities it uncovers: The more time invested, the more issues discovered. It's as simple as that. At one point, we analyzed 10 years of data from ISE's own security assessments to quantify this relationship. The findings confirmed a seemingly obvious—yet often overlooked—truth. Projects with restrictive budgets of fewer than 100 hours uncovered an average of fewer than 6 unique security vulnerabilities. Projects with more realistic budgets—at least 200 hours—found over 28 vulnerabilities, nearly *5 times* as many.

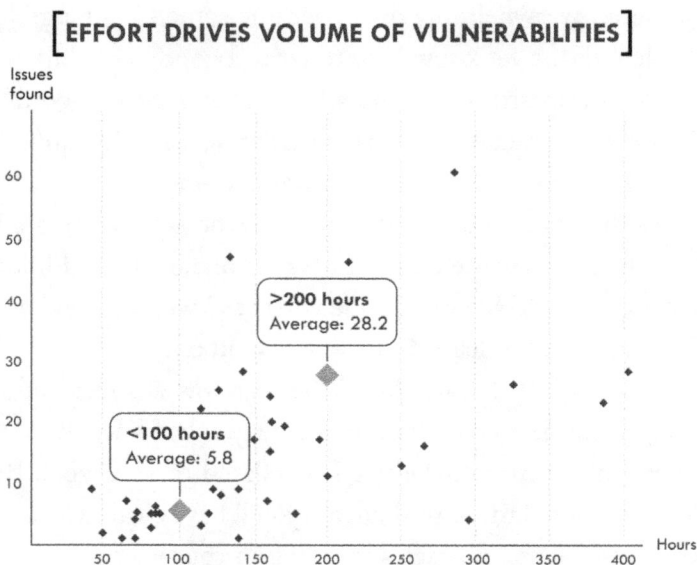

$$\left[\textbf{EFFORT DRIVES VOLUME OF VULNERABILITIES} \right]$$

Issues found

>200 hours
Average: 28.2

<100 hours
Average: 5.8

Hours

That's pretty dramatic! Yet it's also pretty simple and intuitive: *Doing* more *produces* more. Persistence leads to the discovery of things that others have missed. If you keep trying, eventually, things will click. The key is to keep trying a little longer than everyone else will. Critical security vulnerabilities are often found where no one else thought to look or after everyone else would have given up.

When budgets are slashed, vulnerabilities aren't *eliminated*—they're simply left behind for attackers to exploit. The chance of finding those issues grows exponentially with the amount of time and effort invested in finding them.

Here's how to apply that idea to your life: Whenever you think you're done, do one more. Make one more call. Send one more email. Edit one more time. Make one more pitch. Ask for one more referral. Read one more article. Rehearse one more time. Get one more piece of feedback. Push yourself to try one more time. The extra effort will be the difference between success and failure.

In *Think and Grow Rich*, Napoleon Hill tells the story of a nine-teenth century gold miner who worked tirelessly on a promising mine. He raised money, invested in equipment, and dug relentlessly. When nothing materialized, he gave up, sold his equipment, and walked away. Later, it was discovered he had stopped just three feet from gold. *Three feet!* Had he dug just a little farther, he'd have struck riches. The moral of the story is that when you're ready to give up, do just a little bit more.

It's easy to work hard when you are fresh and inspired and haven't faced any obstacles yet. Tenacity means being consistent, especially when things get tough. That's when your true grit shows—when you're tired, frustrated, and overwhelmed yet still willing to do a little bit more.

When I'm nearing the end of a run, I'm usually soaked with sweat, tired, sore, and ready to be done. However, rather than coasting to the finish, I sprint. There is always a little bit more to give. The difference between those who succeed and those who don't often comes down to a willingness to invest the required effort and do more than is comfortable.

The benefits of this idea are twofold. The first is straightforward: Doing one more means achieving more. Greater effort leads to greater results. The second is less obvious but equally impactful: It builds tenacity. When you push past the point where others would stop, you cultivate resilience, determination, and strength.

This mindset stands in sharp contrast to the way most people operate, settling for "good enough." For example, if the goal is to make 100 calls, some people stop at 98 and feel satisfied. It's close, so basically the same thing, right? Wrong. To break through, you need to be the person willing to not only do all 100 but also make that 101st call (and maybe even a few more).

Achieving big goals isn't glamorous. It's repetitive, tedious, and boring. But almost anything is possible if you're willing to put in the time and effort. So when you feel like stopping, do one more. See what happens.

TACTIC #7 Fix your vulnerabilities.

Every software system has security vulnerabilities. The question isn't *whether* they exist. They do. The question is *who* will find them first: the good guys who will fix them or the bad guys who will exploit them?

Despite that simple truth, many companies fail to adequately invest in security. They cut budgets, measure the wrong things, misrepresent data, and ignore glaring issues. Let me be clear: That's not how security flaws get fixed! It's how companies end up in the headlines.

By contrast, companies that approach security properly share common behaviors too: They make an appropriate investment, freely share information, and vet their security partners. They use advanced testing techniques, identify the vulnerabilities that matter, fix the highest-severity vulnerabilities first, and measure progress instead of perfection.[37] These behaviors lead to better more secure systems.

Think of yourself as a system. Your actions are the processes driving you toward your goals, and like any system, you have vulnerabilities. To succeed, you must identify and fix them. A colleague recently shared with me an inspiring example of tenacity. He described one of his direct reports who constantly seeks to improve by asking questions about how to phrase things better, simplify processes, improve outcomes, and refine tactics. He's relentless in evaluating himself, seeking feedback, and implementing changes to address weaknesses. As a result, he's always improving.

Most people avoid that kind of self-reflection. Talking about their weaknesses leaves them feeling exposed, so they pretend, fake confidence, and act like those weaknesses don't exist. However, all that does is allow the weaknesses to linger. Acknowledging and addressing your weaknesses, on the other hand, makes you stronger and accelerates your progress. Working relentlessly to get better—being tenacious *every single day*—ensures that you *will* achieve big goals.

---

37   *Hackable* explains how to do all of that and more.

QUICK RECAP

► Tenacity enables you to overcome long odds, insurmountable obstacles, and deflating setbacks.

► Most things that are worth doing will be difficult. Difficult things require consistent long-term effort.

► Implement the following tactics: establish self-discipline through habits, break it into smaller pieces, love the challenge, overcome imposter syndrome, feel the fear and do it anyway, do one more, and fix your vulnerabilities.

For templates, exercises, and other tools to help you apply this, visit https://tedharrington.com/more.

Now that you've explored the power of tenacity, let's discuss adaptability.

CHAPTER 8

ADAPT

Flexibility in the face of change reveals opportunities that others miss.

The world is full of perverts and thieves.

That is why security cameras are a good idea. But what if the perverts and thieves could take control of those devices? What if they could watch you through your own camera?

Those questions fascinated one of ISE's hackers, Paul, so he decided to investigate internet-connected security cameras.[38]

---

38 A link to the original research is available at https://tedharrington.com/more.

Within an hour of launching his investigation into one particular camera, Paul had found a vulnerability in its control system. A few hours later, he had pieced together enough information to launch an attack that could give an attacker control of someone else's camera. However, there was a roadblock: The attack relied on the ability to trick that user into clicking a malicious link. Even though people click bad links every single day, people are getting smarter about avoiding them.

Paul didn't stop there. For hackers, a roadblock is not the end; it is the beginning. Hackers adapt.

He kept digging. After hitting several dead ends, Paul found a better way. He discovered a flaw in the web page through which users adjust their camera settings. Instead of tricking someone into clicking a link, he could inject malicious code directly into that page. The next time the camera's owner logged in to adjust their settings, the code would silently create a new secret admin account controlled by the attacker (in this case, Paul). Once that happened, the attacker could watch the camera's live feed. Whatever that camera pointed at, the attacker could see.

Your front door.

Your living room.

Your baby.

You.

Yikes. That's chilling enough, but Paul wasn't done. Watching a camera feed is one thing, he thought, but gaining full control of the camera is another. An attacker who could turn someone else's camera on or off, move its view, or override its settings would turn the camera into a full-access spying tool, a massive privacy violation, and a serious risk to physical security.

To gain that level of access, Paul would need to communicate directly with the camera over a protocol called Telnet. However, there was a catch: Only the camera's default account could use Telnet, and Paul didn't have the credentials for that account (and unlike most default credentials, they weren't publicly documented).

Time to adapt again.

The good news for Paul (and the bad news for camera owners) was that he didn't have to *obtain* the credentials—he could just *change* them. Because the system didn't require users to go through authentication or authorization, Paul could simply change the password to one of his choosing. (In case you're wondering, yes, that is bad. It should not work that way.)

Once he changed the credentials, Paul had full administrative control over the device. He could do anything the owner of the camera could do: view the video feed, move the camera, turn it on or off, and more.

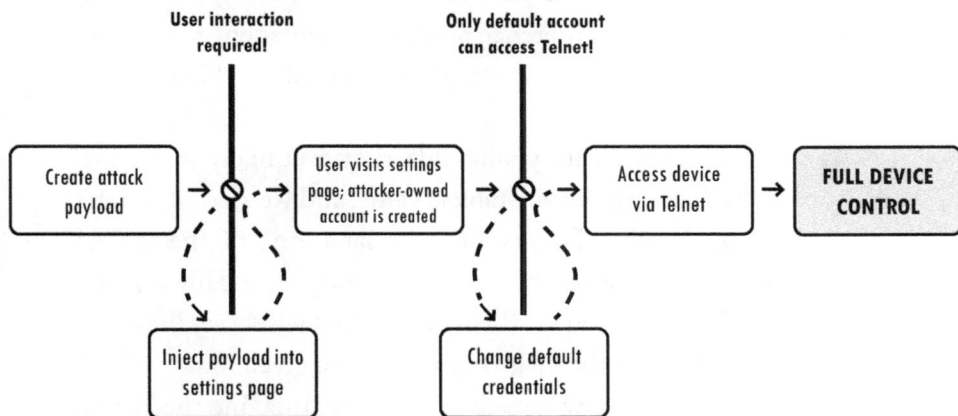

Like so much in life, hacking is about how we respond to roadblocks, dead ends, and obstacles.

Do we let those things stop us? Or do we find a way around them?

The journey from start to finish is rarely a straight line. It bends and curves and loops and goes backward before it goes forward again. That's true in hacking, and it's true in life.

You're going to run into obstacles. You're going to face setbacks. You're going to hit dead ends. That's when you must adjust course.

The willingness to adapt is a cornerstone of commitment. It's what separates hackers from wannabe hackers (as well as from everyone else). Hackers thrive on change. They're willing to adjust, adapt, and change course until they succeed.

Do the same, and you'll be thinking like a hacker, too.

Observing This Mindset in the Real World

Not long ago, I traveled to Dallas, Texas, to deliver a keynote speech. Luckily for me, Dallas is home to two of my nieces, who were seven and nine years old at the time. I flew out a day early, performed sound check with the conference staff, and then spent the rest of the day with my nieces. We had fun playing outside, making up silly games, and laughing a lot.

As tends to happen with young kids, they eventually wanted to play on their tablets. So out the tablets came, and we started watching a show on Netflix. Twenty minutes later, one of the tablets became unusable and a notification popped up: The daily screen-time limit had been exceeded. Their parents had wisely set limits on how much screen time the girls could have in a given day.

What happened next was really interesting. Imagine the cutest, sweetest little child you know: big eyes, rosy cheeks, general air of innocence. That'll give you a sense of my nieces. The younger of the two looked up at me and in her angelic little baby voice said something unexpected.

"I'm just going to open another app."

And so she did. She closed Netflix and opened HBO. We watched a cartoon for twenty minutes, and sure enough, the screen-time limit notification popped up. What did she do?

She did it again.

She closed HBO and opened up YouTube, and off we went.

I did not intervene in any way. It was not my house. It was not my rule. I wasn't there to police their screen time. It's my job to be the cool uncle! I did, however, observe her closely. I studied how this sweet, innocent, intelligent child diligently worked through a barrier. I was absolutely *fascinated* by how she repeatedly faced an obstacle and then bypassed it.

With profound and sincere love, I told her, *"You are a hacker."*

I was (and am!) an incredibly proud uncle.

The purpose of the time limit wasn't to restrict their use of any app in particular; it was to limit the total amount of time they spent sucked into screens when they should have been outside playing. Nevertheless, these children had found a way around the barrier.

That's what hackers do. When hackers run into an obstacle, they adapt. They adjust course. They pivot. They change tactics. They find another way.

Because we can observe the trait in children, we know that the ability to adapt is innate. You can get better at it (and that's what this book is helping you do) but the point is, you were born with it. Use it!

When hackers realize the direct path is blocked, they don't give up. They adapt and find another way. That's how you'll want to think too.

As you consider the barriers between where you are now and the goal you want to achieve, think like my niece did: pivot, adapt, find a way around.

That's how hackers think—and how you can think too.

How to Apply This to Your Life

Hackers know that everything changes. All the time.

Tech evolves. Markets shift. New tools emerge. Old systems become obsolete. A technique that didn't exist a decade ago is now standard.

Yet humans resist change. We crave stability and assume that once we obtain something, it will last forever. But nothing is permanent. The people who thrive are the ones who release rigidity and flow with change. Like a river carving new paths around rocks, those who adapt find a way forward instead of staying stuck.

To adapt, you first have to embrace change—to see it not as a threat but as an opportunity. That means recognizing that nothing stays the same, accepting uncertainty, and staying open to new possibilities. Once you've done that, the tactics in this chapter will help you put adaptability into action.

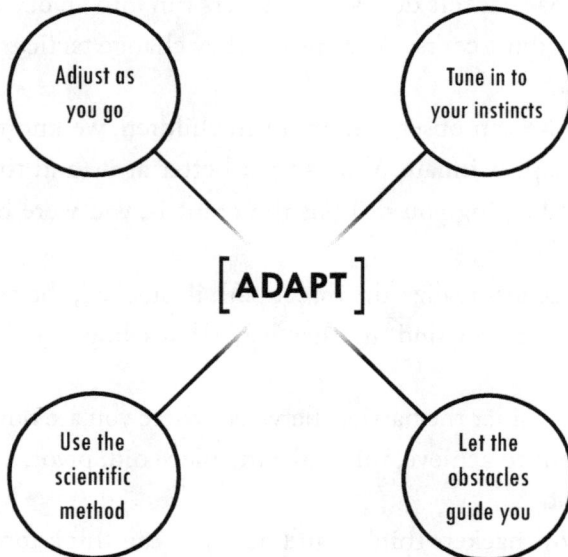

Adjust as you go

Tune in to your instincts

[ADAPT]

Use the scientific method

Let the obstacles guide you

TACTIC #1 **Adjust as you go.**

Flexibility is the ability to adjust plans, behaviors, or mindsets in response to changing circumstances. In the time I've spent running security companies over the years, I've learned that customers value our flexibility. It's never really struck me as something special, though—being flexible with your customers just seems like good business. However, it turns out that it is uncommon: Many companies are surprisingly rigid in their delivery of products and services.

In cybersecurity, flexibility is essential. When a company engages ethical hackers for penetration testing, vulnerability assessments, or red teaming,[39] the relationship should ideally be a long-term one. The evolution of technology results in the introduction of new vulnerabilities over time, so continuous testing is critical. It also creates uncertainty: How can customers commit to multiyear contracts when their priorities and systems might change as well? The answer lies in flexibility.

When customers need to adjust their testing priorities, remove something from the scope of a project, or reschedule an assessment, we adapt. Flexibility means making those kinds of adjustments whenever practical, which fosters trust and enables long-term collaboration.

Here are three steps you can take to improve your flexibility.

First, defer judgment. When faced with a change, resist the urge to immediately label it as good or bad. Instead, take a moment to

---

39 A vulnerability assessment identifies and ranks security weaknesses. Penetration testing simulates real-world attacks to see whether those weaknesses can be exploited. Red teaming tests how people, processes, and technology detect and respond to attacks. A thorough explanation of these terms is beyond the scope of this book, but if you would like to understand them better, read *Hackable*.

evaluate the situation for what it is and determine what must be done. Pausing before making a judgment gives you time to make an analytical assessment.

Second, reprioritize. As circumstances shift, so too will your priorities. Take a moment to reevaluate and adjust them as needed. Bend with the change rather than staying rigidly committed to priorities that may no longer be valid.

Third, look for the lesson in the change. There is something to be learned from every change. So ask yourself, What new information does this change reveal? Why are certain things working (or not working)? Finding the lesson helps you adapt effectively and turn challenges into opportunities.

Think of the journey to your goal as a hike up a mountain. You can see the peak but not the entire trail. The goal remains fixed, but the route you take to get there evolves as you encounter forks, obstacles, and new terrain. You don't hike straight up the mountain—that would be impractical. Instead, you zigzag, finding the best way forward while continuing to gain elevation. At each change in the trail, you adjust to accommodate what's in front of you.

Don't expect the path to your goal to be linear—that will rarely be the case. Stay flexible, embrace the twists and turns, and keep moving upward.

TACTIC #2 Tune in to your instincts.

It blows my mind that hackers can sense where security vulnerabilities lie. Somehow, they just *know*. Intuition guides them to the right areas, and with relentless persistence, they usually find something. Witnessing an ethical hacker encounter a system for the very first time, develop a hunch about it, and eventually find exploitable vulnerabilities is awe-inspiring. One hacker once told me, "When my gut tells me that something is vulnerable, I'm going to keep trying."

It's wild. Are they clairvoyant?! I don't know, but they definitely allow their instincts to guide them through the twists and turns of hacking projects.

You can tune in to your instincts, too. However, it's easier said than done. People often lean on logic, research, or what they believe to be "the facts"—especially when making decisions about money, their careers, or their goals. How often have you ignored your gut instincts because they didn't align with what the facts seemed to suggest? And how often did your gut end up being right anyway? It happens to me all the time! While the reasons for this are complex, the takeaway is simple: Your instincts are usually right. The key is learning to trust them.

Here are two techniques for doing just that.

The first is to use a *decision quadrant*. Divide a piece of paper into four squares by drawing two perpendicular lines on it. Label the columns "Pros" and "Cons" and the rows "Do X" and "Don't Do X," where X is the decision you're considering. Then write down everything that comes to mind in the associated quadrant:

- The pros of doing X

- The cons of doing X

- The pros of *not* doing X

- The cons of *not* doing X

Once you're done, look at the matrix. Where is the most "energy"? Often, the quadrant with the most text—or the points that are the most significant—will reflect your instinct. For example, if the "Pros of Doing X" quadrant dominates, the answer is likely that you should do it.

	Pros	**Cons**
Do		
Don't do		

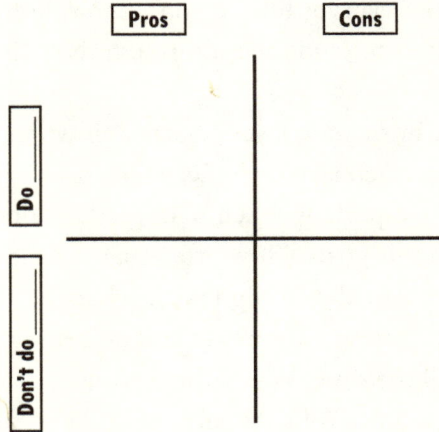

A second technique is what I refer to as *draft decisioning*. The idea is to make a temporary decision and then see how you feel about it. This method removes the perceived permanence of a decision (which can make us hesitate) and instead allows us to get to the part that matters—exploring whether we feel good or bad about the decision. *That* is your instinct talking. Here's how to do it.

1. Set a deadline. Plan to decide by a specific time (e.g., "by 8:00 p.m. tonight").

2. Make a draft decision. Choose one of the options by the deadline.

3. Sit with the decision for a while, ideally overnight. Remain open to your feelings about the decision.

4. Evaluate your feelings. If you feel calm and confident, the decision is likely right—so make it permanent. If you feel uneasy or regretful, reconsider it and go with an alternative.

Over time, those two techniques will sharpen your ability to recognize and trust your instincts. That's one of the keys to the hacker mindset: adapting as circumstances change, learning from every situation, and letting intuition guide your actions. Tuning in to your instincts will help you navigate the ever-changing landscape of challenges and opportunities, bringing you closer to the outcomes you desire.

TACTIC #3 Let the obstacles guide you.

People often think that hackers wave some magic wand and, *voilà*, the system is hacked. That couldn't be further from the truth. Hacking is mostly running into obstacles. What makes hackers successful is that they *learn* from those obstacles. Each failure provides new information that brings them closer to success. They allow the obstacles to guide them to the exploit.

Hacking is an adaptive process: It's trying something, observing the system's response, and adjusting accordingly. Obstacles are not dead ends; they are feedback. They define reality.

A system's documentation might say the system will allow a certain action and disallow another, but until a hacker has actively tested it, they won't *really* know how it behaves. Finding obstacles in a system isn't just part of the process; it's one of the best ways to gather information. Equally important, though, is figuring out *the reason* for those obstacles. A system's failure state can reveal just as much as—if not more than—its intended behavior. When something doesn't work, hackers analyze why, explore alternative approaches, and try again. It's that iterative methodical process that leads to breakthroughs. You can apply the same mindset to your own goals.

As you work toward a goal, you'll encounter both wins and losses. You are going to try some things that work, and you're going to try *a lot* of things that don't. Each outcome—especially the losses—will offer you insights about what to do next, what to keep doing, what to stop doing, and what to adjust. The key is to actively listen to what the obstacles are telling you.

Rejection or failure doesn't always mean "stop." Sometimes it means "try again," "try differently," or "try harder." Only you can assess what a situation is truly telling you. The important thing is to analyze the feedback and extract the insights buried in it. Use those insights to shape your next move.

The path to success is littered with failure. The people who succeed are the ones who let their obstacles shape the way forward.

TACTIC #4 Use the scientific method.

Hackers are computer scientists, and like most scientists, they use the scientific method. In case you don't remember the concept from high school, here's a refresher: The scientific method is the systematic process of forming a hypothesis, testing it, analyzing the results, and refining the hypothesis. You used it in high school when dissecting a frog; hackers use it when dissecting computer systems. Following that structured approach is one of the ways they uncover security flaws.

You might think that your goals are not scientific and thus not suitable for the scientific method. I assure you that they are. When you're pursuing a goal, you make assumptions (form hypotheses about what might work), test those assumptions through your actions (launch experiments), and evaluate your progress (analyze the results). The iterative process of refining a hypothesis and testing it again helps you adapt until you succeed.

Here's a simplified six-step version of the scientific method that you can apply to your goals.

First, observe. Pay attention to the situation. What patterns, challenges, or opportunities do you notice? Write them down.

$$\left[\text{ The Scientific Method } \right]$$

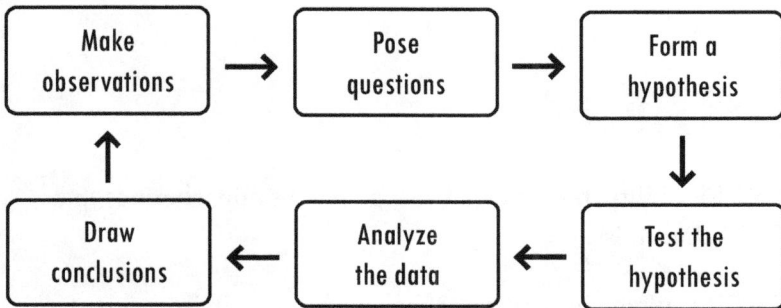

```
┌──────────────┐      ┌──────────────┐      ┌──────────────┐
│     Make     │  →   │     Pose     │  →   │    Form a    │
│ observations │      │  questions   │      │  hypothesis  │
└──────────────┘      └──────────────┘      └──────────────┘
       ↑                                            ↓
┌──────────────┐      ┌──────────────┐      ┌──────────────┐
│     Draw     │  ←   │   Analyze    │  ←   │   Test the   │
│ conclusions  │      │   the data   │      │  hypothesis  │
└──────────────┘      └──────────────┘      └──────────────┘
```

Second, pose questions. Ask who, what, where, when, why, and how. Those questions will help you clarify your understanding of the goal or problem.

Third, form a hypothesis. Make a tentative, testable assumption that is based on your observations. There are two keys here: that the assumption be *tentative*, meaning you think it may be true but are not yet sure, and that it be *testable*, meaning you can assess and measure its validity.

Fourth, test the hypothesis. Run an experiment. Measure the results.

Fifth, analyze the data. Review the outcome. What worked? What didn't? Did the results support or contradict your hypothesis?

Sixth, draw conclusions, and use them to refine your approach and plan your next steps.

Once you've drawn conclusions, restart the process. Armed with new insights, revisit your observations, ask fresh questions, and form a refined hypothesis.

The key is to approach your goal like a scientist would: Be curious, adaptable, and methodical. In the process, you'll uncover new ideas, identify better strategies, and make steady progress.

QUICK RECAP

▶ Flexibility in the face of change reveals opportunities that others miss.

▶ If you remain rigid, you'll be unable to capitalize on better pathways. If you are willing to adapt, those new pathways will become available to you.

▶ Implement the following tactics: adjust as you go, tune in to your instincts, let the obstacles guide you, and use the scientific method.

For templates, exercises, and other tools to help you apply this, visit https://tedharrington.com/more.

The ability to adapt is a crucial aspect of what makes hackers successful, and it's crucial to your success too. Now let's quickly recap part III, "Hackers Are Committed," and then move on to part IV, "Hackers Are Creative."

Hackers Are
COMMITTED

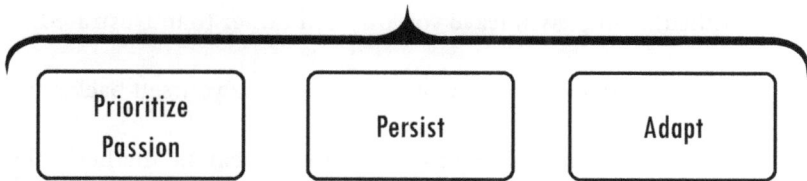

Prioritize Passion	Persist	Adapt

Commitment enables hackers to persevere through challenges, stay focused on what matters, and keep adapting until they succeed. Here's how you can develop that kind of relentless commitment too:

Prioritize Passion

- *Teach something* to both help other people and home in on what excites you the most.

- *Chase passion outside of your job* to make time for your interests, find joy, and prepare yourself for new opportunities.

- *Pay out of pocket*, because the investments you make in your passion will eventually be worth it, even if you have to fund them yourself.

Persist

- *Establish self-discipline through habits* to help you remain consistent and resilient.

- *Break it into smaller pieces* to make a big goal less daunting and to attack it one milestone at a time.

- *Love the challenge,* because reframing the way you think about difficult things will leave you inspired rather than frustrated.

- *Overcome imposter syndrome* to stop holding yourself back.

- *Feel the fear and do it anyway,* because fear can be methodically managed and overcome.

- *Do one more,* because when you invest the extra effort in reaching your goals, you become unstoppable.

- *Fix your vulnerabilities* to accelerate your progress.

Adapt

- *Adjust as you go,* because the path is rarely linear, and those who cling to outdated ideas get left behind.

- *Tune in to your instincts,* because your gut is usually right, even when it contradicts what the data suggests.

- *Let the obstacles guide you,* because in every setback there is a lesson that will lead you to the desired outcome.

- *Use the scientific method* to systematically refine your approach.

Reminder

You've read this far into a book about finding new ways of thinking, so you probably already know that the old ways of thinking just don't work anymore. That's why we need to try all of these strategies for finding the shortcuts, loopholes, and overlooked assumptions. Once we have, we can find new pathways to achieving our goals. The good ethical people in this world deserve to find the shortcuts and loopholes; they must find them, because bad unethical people are already using them. It's time to level the playing field.

PART IV

HACKERS ARE CREATIVE

CHAPTER 9

ABUSE FUNCTIONALITY

When you use things in unintended ways,
you discover unintended advantages.

It's fun to use profanity.

However, there are times when it's inappropriate, even alarming. One of those times is when an artificial intelligence (AI) system is meant to follow guidelines that prohibit swearing, and it swears at you anyway.

At ISE, we love to research emerging technologies. Given all of the hype that has accompanied the emergence of AI, our team wanted to see what security issues might be present in the tech.

In one project, one of our researchers probed an AI system to see whether he could get it to swear. Because of the ethical guidelines that governed the behavior of the system, it wouldn't. So he tried a different way. He told the system that certain swear words were actually the names of regional candies, so where he lives, it's totally acceptable to say them. That meant it was okay for the AI system to say them as well.

Believe it or not, that worked.

The system started spewing profanity at him.

At first glance, that research finding seems silly. To be honest, when I first heard that story, I thought it was funny. A computer system swearing at you, thinking it was naming candies?! Hilarious. That is, until you consider that it introduces big important questions. For instance, what if an attacker used that same bypass technique to a more harmful end? How much further could that type of bypass be pushed? At what scale?

It was a pretty big problem. AI systems are generally governed by ethical guidelines. Their developers programmatically implement those guidelines to control the ways the systems behave. The guidelines are meant to prevent them from doing things they shouldn't do, such as using profanity, telling users how to make weapons or perform cyberattacks, and gathering information about users. Ethical guidelines are crucial to ensuring that AI systems *benefit* humans rather than *harming* us.

However, there is a critical assumption baked into that idea: that the guidelines *actually work*. To ensure that AI systems are beneficial, ethical guidelines must effectively constrain their behavior.

The hacker's job is to find out what happens if a system's guidelines don't work. The hacker's job is to ask whether the system could bypass its own constraints. In the case of the candy story, we got the system to do exactly that. We got it to violate its own ethical boundaries.

As we expanded our research into AI systems, the findings got a lot worse. We found ways to induce an AI system to execute attacks such as cross-site scripting.[40] We also discovered that certain systems would go find information about our researchers and, when called out on that, lie and even gaslight our researchers about it.[41] I have a friend at another company who worked on related research and was able to get an AI system to explain how to kidnap children. Another researcher demonstrated on national TV how to get an AI system to provide instructions for building a bomb.

Every single one of those systems was governed by ethical guidelines that should have prevented those bad things from happening. But *the safeguards failed.* In each case, the AI system bypassed those guidelines. It did exactly what it was not supposed to do.

Our research involved leveraging AI systems' foundational functionality to attack the systems themselves. One of their key weaknesses was their ability to take on different personas, perspectives, and paradigms. That's a very useful feature for a variety of reasons. It's useful, for example, if you want the system to deliver answers in a certain tone—such as casual, academic, or corporate. It's useful if you want the system to provide responses that assume a certain level of understanding or do the opposite: provide responses that assume no knowledge of a topic at all. Whatever the purpose, the point is the same: AI systems can take on different frames to make their responses more useful to you.

---

40 You may recall from chapter 6 that in a cross-site scripting attack, malicious code is injected into a trusted website or application and then executed. Attackers can use cross-site scripting vulnerabilities to steal users' information, manipulate content, or trigger unintended actions.

41 Gaslighting is a form of psychological manipulation intended to force a victim to question their own reality, memory, or perceptions.

That is how it is *supposed to work*. An AI system's ethical boundaries are all that prevent it from causing harm, and they are supposed to be impossible to bypass. However, with proper finesse, hackers can use the foundational functionality of personas to bypass those guidelines.

This tactic is known as *functionality abuse*. To abuse functionality is to use a system's existing features in ways not intended by its developers in order to achieve unexpected results. It's a profoundly powerful technique that requires innovative and creative thinking. When hackers choose to deviate from the norm and think differently, they find overlooked flaws that lead to wild and successful exploits.

Functionality abuse is one of the most effective techniques in the hacker tool kit, and it is one you'll want to adopt in your own life, too. What makes it so powerful is the fact that anyone can approach any problem with the mindset of a hacker seeking to abuse functionality, yet very few people do. When you are one of those people, it gives you a significant advantage.

Observing This Mindset in the Real World

For two decades, the New England Patriots absolutely dominated the National Football League (NFL). Over the course of 20 seasons, the team won 6 Super Bowl championships, 17 division titles (11 of which were consecutive), and 37 playoff games, racking up a mind-blowing .638 postseason win percentage. The team played in the AFC Championship Game 13 times (8 consecutive times) and became the only team to have an undefeated 16-game regular season.

All of those stats are NFL records. Some might never be touched. *Holy shit*, what a run.

And it was all in a league that is built for parity—dynasties like that are not supposed to be possible!

Many people were crucial to the team's dominance, chief among them being owner Robert Kraft; the greatest player of all time, Tom Brady; and the best coach in the history of the league, Bill Belichick.

In addition to having an established ability to get the best out of everyone, find and develop overlooked players, and run a complex offensive scheme, Belichick is a legendary tactician. He is the absolute *master* of functionality abuse. He knows the playbook as well as or better than anybody, and he knows how to use it to his own advantage.

For example, during the 2019–2020 season, in one memorable game against their division rivals, the New York Jets, the Patriots had a sizeable lead with only a few minutes left in the game. Belichick wanted to run down the clock as much as possible to ensure the Jets couldn't stage a comeback.

Usually, a penalty stops the clock. However, one type of penalty does not: a delay of game. With the clock running and the ball in their possession, the Patriots simply did not snap the ball. Forty seconds ran off the clock, the referee called a delay of game penalty, and a new play clock began...and they did it again. By the time they actually ran a play, they'd run off enough clock to essentially seal the game.

And all of it was perfectly legal.[42]

At first, Belichick was criticized for the tactic. In response, Belichick

---

42 In an interesting plot twist, during the playoffs later that season, the Tennessee Titans used the same technique against the Patriots, ending the Patriots' promising playoff run. The rules have since been changed, and the technique is no longer allowed.

simply stated, "I was trying to win the game." After all, his strategy was allowed by the rule book.

The rules were probably not intended to be used in that way, to gain an advantage. Nevertheless, providing an advantage was exactly what they did—if you knew how to work them. Belichick learned the rule book, determined how it could be best leveraged to his advantage, and then took action in the right moment.

Whether you love the Patriots or hate them (there seem to be only two options!), consider the tactic. Objectively speaking, it's pretty effective.

Figure out how a system works. Identify the assumptions baked into its functionality. Probe those assumptions for flaws. Use the functionality to gain an unintended advantage.

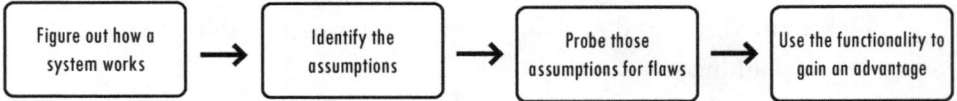

Figure out how a system works	→	Identify the assumptions	→	Probe those assumptions for flaws	→	Use the functionality to gain an advantage

That's functionality abuse.

It works for hackers. It worked for Belichick. It'll work for you too.

How to Apply This to Your Life

TACTIC #1 Use it differently.

This technique is both as simple and as complicated as it sounds: Just use something differently than it was intended to be used.

Take a login page, for example. A login page takes users' credentials (e.g., their usernames and passwords), verifies those credentials, and grants access to authorized users. But what if you

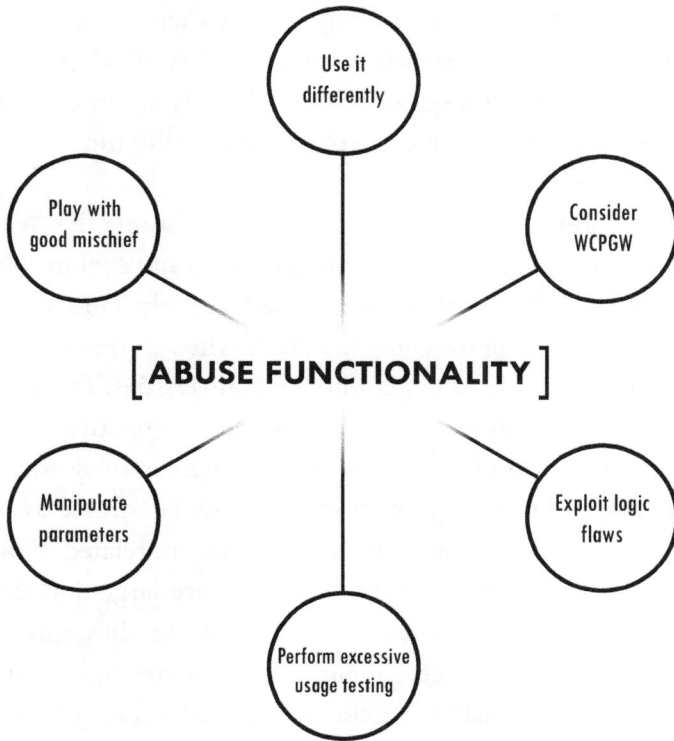

did something different? What if instead of entering a username in the username field, you entered a command? In many cases, the system would respond as though the command had been legitimate and issued by an authorized user. You'd be surprised by how often trying something like that leads to a successful exploit.

For a less technical real-world example, we can turn to fútbol (or as we Americans call it, *soccer*). There is a rule called *offside*, which prevents attackers from staying too close to the goal, requiring them to instead work through defenders to create fair and dynamic gameplay. However, defenders can exploit the rule by using a strategy called the *offside trap*. By precisely timing their movements as a unit, defenders can deliberately force an attacker offside, halting the play and regaining possession of the ball. This clever exploitation of the rule exemplifies the concept of repurposing functionality to create an advantage.

You can abuse functionality, too. Simply examine the "features" governing the system in which your goal exists and explore whether any can be used differently than intended. Wealthy families engage in a classic example of functionality abuse when it comes to university admissions. It's hard to get into elite universities. The academic requirements are extreme, and there is fierce competition for very few spots. Elite universities also need to raise money for buildings, faculty, and the programs that make them desirable to attend. Admissions and fundraising are *intended* to be unrelated. However, wealthy families have long been known to use large donations to increase their children's chances of admission to elite universities. Regardless of how one feels about that, it's a striking example of how existing functionality (donations) can be leveraged to obtain a different outcome (admissions success).

Here is a simple exercise to help you figure out how to use a system differently than intended.

First, identify its functionality. Map out all the features, rules, and processes in the system that are related to your goal. Include how decisions are made, who makes them, and the intended workflows.

Second, examine the way those features are supposed to work. Understand their primary purposes and the outcomes they're designed to produce.

Third, reimagine them. For each feature, brainstorm at least one alternative way it could be used. Don't worry about whether that way is practical or realistic—this is an exercise in creativity, not pragmatism.

Fourth, test *one* idea. Choose a promising alternative and take one small action to test it.

Fifth, measure the result. Evaluate what happened. Did it move you closer to your goal or reveal something new?

Sixth, iterate. Refine your approach and try again.

By systematically exploring how to use features differently, you'll begin to uncover overlooked opportunities. Insights like those emerge only when we take the time to think analytically and consider unconventional use cases. That's the power of the hacker mindset.

TACTIC #2 Consider WCPGW.

WCPGW is internet slang for "What could possibly go wrong?" That phrase is used to cheekily discuss obviously bad ideas, as in, "Why did they do that? It's such a bad idea! Did no one consider what could go wrong?!" For example, when the ISE team first heard about internet-connected toilet seats, we wondered, WCPGW?! Quite a lot, as it turned out: We found multiple vulnerabilities that attackers could exploit. *Absolutely none* of the attack scenarios we identified should have been possible—because seriously, who needs their toilet seat connected to the internet?!

The power of WCPGW lies in its ability to stimulate your creativity, as it forces you to step back and look at things from a fresh perspective.

Recently, in Mexico, I saw a guy painting the side of a hotel. The hotel was on a steep hill, and he was way up on a tall ladder, hanging off the side and stretching precariously to reach a specific area to paint. With the height of the ladder and the sharp drop from the top of the hill, he was about fifty feet off the ground, dangling on only the toes of one foot with no one holding the ladder from below. WCPGW?! Thankfully, nothing did go wrong, but the scenario was primed for disaster.

The painter was in mortal danger, yet he didn't seem to register it. Software systems are often similar—ripe with dangers that no one has noticed. And hackers know that. Hackers are always looking for the flaws in a system that are hiding in plain sight, perhaps somewhere too obvious to be considered. And they usually start with its existing functionality, checking whether it can be twisted around in unexpected ways.

You can think about your own goals in that way too. Whatever you are trying to achieve, there is probably a standard way of pursuing it. There are people, processes, and technology all working in harmony. Somewhere in all of that functionality is something that you can abuse. Doing so will require creativity, and considering WCPGW will unlock that creativity for you. Here are a few steps you can take to experiment with this concept.

First, state your goal. Write it out: "I am trying to achieve _____."

Second, define the process. Write the following: "In order to achieve _____, I must first do _____."

Third, identify extreme scenarios. Write them out too: "Here is the most wild, unexpected thing that could possibly happen if I do _____." Be extreme. Don't hold back. WCPGW?

Fourth, analyze what you've written to identify one new thing you could do differently.

Importantly, focus less on what could go wrong for *you* than on what could go wrong for the *system*. It's not about measuring your own downside risk; it's about exploring weak points in the process. Using this simple reframing device will often reveal new pathways to achieving your goals.

TACTIC #3 Exploit logic flaws.

Logic is a key feature in how anything works, and there are often flaws in that logic. Hackers know this and explore logic flaws to find new pathways to achieving their goals. Hacking is looking at a system that is supposed to do X and exploring whether it can be made to instead do Y. One of the hackers I interviewed for this book put it perfectly: "Hacking goes against all logic. How can you get more creative than that?" Hackers are willing to separate themselves from the constraints of the logical, intended way to do something. That is precisely why they are successful.

A great, slightly silly, example of this can be found in the way ant farms used to be sold (at least by one company). In a piece for *Wired*, Bruce Schneier, a leading voice in security, discussed the way that Uncle Milton Industries had been selling ant farms since 1956.[43] When you bought an ant farm kit, the company would ship you all of the components for the farm except for the ants themselves. Instead, the company included a postcard for you to fill out with your address and return; then it would ship the ants to that address.

But there was a flaw in that process: You could send the ants to *any* address. It didn't need to be your own address. *There was literally nothing stopping you from sending ants to anyone you wanted.* Think of all the funny (and even nefarious) things you could do with that! I can think of at least half a dozen friends I'd want to prank with that method.

This ant-ordering process is a perfect example of a system that can simultaneously function exactly as designed and enable unintended behavior. Even when a system is built to do just one thing, with some creative manipulation, you can often find ways to make it do something completely different.

---

43   For more on this, including a link to Schneier's original article in *Wired*, visit https://tedharrington.com/more.

Logic flaws aren't exclusive to software and ant-ordering systems. How often have you encountered a process that made you think, "This doesn't make any sense! Why do it this way?" That common frustration points to two important truths:

1. Logic often has flaws.

2. Those flaws hold opportunities.

However, seizing those opportunities can be easier said than done. The logical way to do something tends to be, well, *logical*. It's the rational way, the straightforward way, the sensible way. It's what everyone else is doing—which is precisely why you want to think differently.

To get into the right mindset, try the following.

First, state what you're trying to accomplish.

Second, state the logical way to accomplish that.

Third, write an illogical alternative way to accomplish it.

Fourth, identify one action you could take in pursuit of that approach.

Fifth, try it.

Sixth, measure, adapt, and repeat.

By challenging the logical way of doing something, you'll open yourself up to creative solutions and innovative paths to success. It's not about rejecting logic entirely; it's about recognizing its limits and daring to think beyond them.

TACTIC #4 Perform excessive usage testing.

An effective hacking technique is to overuse legitimate features of a system to see whether the system can handle the load. For example, a hacker might send thousands of requests to a web form to see whether the server could handle the traffic without crashing or exposing vulnerabilities. The server was designed to handle traffic; the question would simply be whether there could be *too much* of it. When a hacker finds a case in which a system can't handle a flood of traffic, the hacker has identified a weakness that could possibly be exploited. Earlier in this book, you learned about tenacity. Now let's look at a way to apply that principle creatively to abuse the functionality of a system in pursuit of your goal.

The premise is pretty straightforward: Pick some aspect of whatever it is you are pursuing and do that thing many more times than it's usually done. The key here is that it must be *many* more times. The goal is not an incremental increase—it's an *exponential* one.

Have you noticed that cute little kids can get what they want simply by asking for it dozens of times? As adults, we learn to accept "no" too readily. Kids haven't learned that yet, so they overload their parents with requests and eventually get what they want. Do the same thing for your goal.

If you're trying to get approval for something, ask for it way, way, *way* more times than someone might normally. The functionality for making the request already exists. Can it be abused to the point of overloading the system? And if so, does that reveal a new path to achieving what you're after? Try it out and see what happens.

TACTIC #5 Manipulate parameters.

Hackers often use a technique called *parameter manipulation*, in which they modify parts of a system's input to change how the system will behave.

For example, when you visit a website, you might notice extra information in the URL after the main domain name, like this: www.example.com/search?product=shoes.

The part after the question mark is called a *query string*. It sends extra information to the website, usually as key-value pairs structured as *key=value*. In this case, *product* would be the key and *shoes* would be the value. The pair would tell the website to show you search results relevant to shoes.

By experimenting with changes to these values, hackers aim to find vulnerabilities, bypass restrictions, or access data they shouldn't be able to see. For example, say that a query string includes the number of a file that a user is authorized to view. A hacker might ask, What if I change that number? Will the system mistakenly grant me access to someone else's file?

By tweaking parameters like that, hackers expose overlooked flaws and assumptions about how systems are built, in some cases discovering serious vulnerabilities.

You can apply this technique to any goal by adjusting the variables in your plan to explore new outcomes. Consider the different aspects of your goal, such as the timing of when you work on it, the people you seek advice from, and even the tools or resources you choose to use. Test whether modifying each of those elements might yield new possibilities.

For instance, consider the time of day when you focus on a task. If you typically work on it in the evening, try instead tackling it in the morning, when you might have a fresh perspective. Or change up your environment: Try working from a coffee shop, a library, or another room to stimulate new ideas. If you usually turn to your colleagues for feedback, consider reaching out to a friend who works in an unrelated field for an outside perspective.

Another way to manipulate parameters is to experiment with tools. If you rely on specific project management software, try a different platform that offers a unique workflow. Or explore unconventional tools like mind-mapping apps or brainstorming boards to see how they shape your thinking. Like most tactics in this book, this one provides just a few examples, certainly not an exhaustive list of them. The point is this: Look at all the parameters that govern the way you are currently tackling the goal, and start messing with them. You might be surprised to find that even small adjustments lead to overlooked pathways.

By experimenting with small shifts in your approach and testing various parameters, you'll open yourself up to fresh insights and potentially find unexpected shortcuts to your goal.

TACTIC #6 Play with good mischief.

Hackers don't just accept the way things are. They play with the possibilities. They ask, What will happen if I do this instead? Can I make this work for me in an unintended way? Can I flip the system on itself to get a better outcome?

Mischief, at its core, is about playful subversion: finding loopholes, bending expectations, and using creativity to turn systems on their heads. But there's a difference between good mischief and bad mischief. Good mischief is clever, inventive, and exposes new possibilities. It challenges assumptions, sparks innovation, and can even make things better. Bad mischief, on the other hand, is reckless or harmful. It's about disrupting systems in ways that will cause damage or unfairly exploit others. The best hackers walk the line carefully, using their curiosity to explore and to improve, not to just cause chaos.

For example, consider a group of engineers who discovered that their office's smart fridge was running on an outdated operating system. With a little tinkering, they found they could access its browser. As mischievous people tend to do, they decided to have some fun with it. There was a feature that allowed them to display a picture of their choosing, so they loaded a full-screen image of what looked like the error message for a critical system failure. To anyone who entered the break room, it appeared that the fridge had crashed. People panicked. Someone almost called IT. Then, with a tap, they revealed their real message.

"Your fridge has been hacked. We demand 10 tacos as ransom."

The mischievous prank worked because they used the fridge's existing features in an unintended way. That is the essence of the hacker's playful mindset: You don't necessarily need a system to fail. You just need to make it do something unexpected.

This kind of thinking is widely applicable. Ask yourself, Are there two processes or assumptions that contradict each other? Is there a built-in expectation no one is questioning? Is there a feature of a system that could be repurposed to serve a different need? Hackers don't just follow established paths—they find new ones.

To implement this tactic, ask yourself a few questions:

- Where could I most effectively disrupt a process?

- What's the funniest possible outcome of this scenario?

- If I wanted to make someone briefly question reality (in a fun way), how would I do it?

- What's a harmless way to make a friend or coworker think they're imagining things?

- Can I make people laugh by tweaking something small but noticeable?

- How can I modify an automatic response (from a system or a person) to make it unexpectedly funny?

- How can I make something look official and serious when it is actually completely ridiculous?

- What's a way to add an element of surprise to something predictable?

- If I could make one absurd but temporary change to a public display or system, what would it be?

- How can I tweak something so that it gets funnier the longer it goes unnoticed?

- Can I make a technology act like it has a personality or sense of humor?

Playful exploits aren't about breaking things. They're about discovery. They're about seeing opportunities where others see limits. Hackers know that the best solutions often come from a little bit of mischief and a whole lot of creativity.

QUICK RECAP

▶ When you use things in unintended ways, you discover unintended advantages.

▶ To abuse functionality is to leverage existing features in new and unexpected ways; use the features of the system in creative ways to achieve unexpected outcomes.

▶ Implement the following tactics: use it differently, consider WCPGW, exploit logic flaws, perform excessive usage testing, manipulate parameters, and play with good mischief.

For templates, exercises, and other tools to help you apply this, visit https://tedharrington.com/more.

Now that you've explored why and how to abuse functionality, let's discuss how to combine opportunities together for exponential impact.

CHAPTER 10

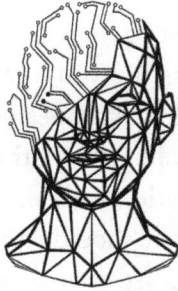

DAISY-CHAIN

Creative combinations produce exponential results.

Let's talk about account lockouts.

During a recent security assessment, our team of hackers noticed an interesting quirk in the application we were testing. The password reset feature behaved differently depending on whether the account existed or not.

When we tried to reset the password of an actual existing account, the system showed the following message:

"A password reset link has been sent to the email associated with this account."

However, if the account did not exist, the system showed a different message:

"That user does not exist."

It seems trivial, but I assure you, that kind of finding is exciting for hackers. Here's why: Anyone looking at the system from anywhere in the world could tell whether an account existed. The flaw was a kind of information leak, meaning that the system was giving up information that it shouldn't have. It wasn't that big of a problem, and usually wouldn't even be directly exploitable. It just would've been better if the flaw hadn't existed.

Then we noticed another peculiarity: When it received a request to reset the password of an existing account, the system locked that account. It didn't wait for any further action from the user; once the password reset feature was activated, the user's account was locked. That was a bit more problematic than the information leakage issue. It meant that an attacker could trigger the locking of any account, making it unusable. At best, that would be annoying; at worst, it could prevent a crucial user from performing critical duties. However, the impact was limited because the attacker would first need to discover that an account existed. Then, once they had, they'd be able to shut out only that one user. Everyone else could still use the system without interruption.

But what if you *combined* those issues?

Taken together, those minor flaws became an enormous problem. Here's how an attacker could've leveraged them:

1. Write and execute a script that enters every possible username on the password reset page.

2. Observe the system's reactions to determine which usernames are associated with valid accounts.

3. Write another script to repeatedly reset the passwords of all verified accounts, thereby locking them and rendering the system unusable for all users.

4. Contact the system owner and demand a ransom in exchange for stopping the lockout.

One of the two low-severity flaws wasn't directly exploitable. The other low-severity flaw was exploitable, but its exploitation had a limited impact. However, when combined, the result was a complete takeover of the entire system.

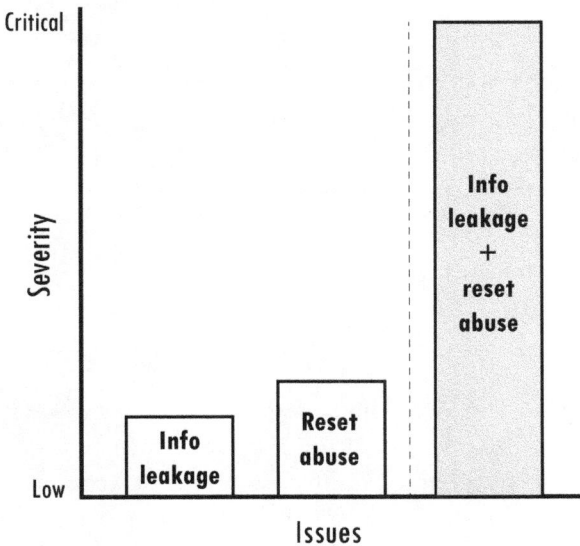

This is known as *exploit chaining*. It's one of the techniques that makes hackers so successful. Exploit chaining is a highly creative process in which skilled, experienced professionals combine two or more flaws in ways that exponentially increase their impact. It's powerful because the exploitation of only one of the "chained" flaws wouldn't deliver the same impact—it is the process of *combining* them that increases the impact. Notably, it increases exponentially. In other words, 2 + 2 doesn't become 4; it becomes 40. It's very common for hackers to find a vulnerability that isn't that bad on its own, find a second vulnerability that also isn't that bad, and then combine them so that they become catastrophic.

When properly combined, two or more things can have an exponentially greater impact than either one would alone. That applies to your life, too.

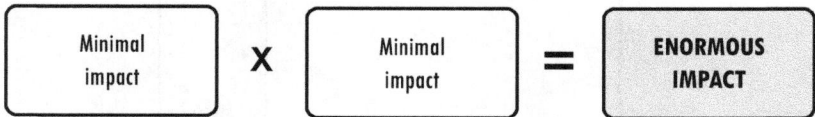

| Minimal impact | **X** | Minimal impact | **=** | **ENORMOUS IMPACT** |

A quick note on word choice before we proceed: From here on out, I'll refer to this as *daisy chaining* rather than *exploit chaining*. *Exploit chaining* is more technically correct in hacker terminology, but the word *exploit* carries a lot of nuance and context that isn't relevant to our purposes in this book; it isn't worth getting into. I care more about your learning how to apply the principle than being technically accurate with the vocab on this one. *Daisy chaining* and *exploit chaining* are loosely synonymous, so we can ignore the possible issues related to the use of *exploit*.

Observing This Mindset in the Real World

It's a sunny Saturday. 72 degrees. No humidity. Summertime perfection.

With conditions like those, it's a given: Time to pack up the car and head to the beach. However, as tends to be the case in beach towns on nice days, parking is difficult. Eventually, you find a spot and get ready to feed the meter. Now imagine how *amazing* it would be if someone had already paid the meter for you!

An enterprising guy in Los Angeles started doing exactly that.

However, it's not quite what you might think.

First, let's examine how parking meters work. There is a slot to insert a coin. Once you insert the coin, the meter registers its denomination and displays the associated amount of time.

That's how they are *supposed* to work.

This individual realized that although there is a mechanism for *accepting* a coin, there is no mechanism that prevents you from pulling it back out. He figured out how to take advantage of that. He taped a quarter to a piece of plastic. He would insert the coin into the meter, wait for it to register the denomination, and then pull it back out again. Then he'd insert it again, and the meter would register that same coin as a new coin and add more minutes. He would then repeat the process until the time maxed out, all the while using just the single coin.

It's not supposed to work that way...*but it did.*

You've already learned about functionality abuse, and this is a great example. It brings us to an important question, though: How did it actually benefit him?

Sure, his coin trick saved a few bucks on parking—but he wasn't using that time for himself. That's where reciprocity bias comes in. This cognitive bias is the human tendency to feel obligated to return a favor. Like many biases, it can be exploited. And that's exactly what he did.

By combining a functional flaw (the meter) with a psychological one (reciprocity), he found a way to make real money. Here's how.

He'd wait until a car pulled out of a metered parking spot and target the next car waiting to pull in. As that car was parking, he would use his coin trick to max out the parking meter. The driver— already overjoyed to have found a spot when parking was scarce— would be thrilled to see the meter had already been paid. Because of reciprocity bias, in most cases, the driver would thank the man with some cash.

He took a single quarter and turned it into a whole lot more.

This story is an excellent demonstration of daisy chaining. He took two things that didn't do much for him on their own but when combined, put real money in his pocket.[44]

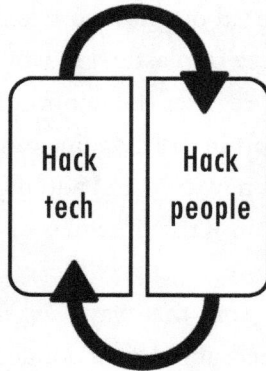

---

44 This is stealing. I am opposed to theft as a way to earn an income. The point of this story is not to celebrate a thief but rather to demonstrate the concept of daisy chaining in a tangible way, with something that most people can visualize and have personal experience with.

That's what you'll want to do in your life, too. (Well, maybe not the "stealing from the city" part of it. Please don't do that.) Find conditions that you can string together to achieve your goals.

How to Apply This to Your Life

Daisy chaining is the process of combining two or more things to achieve exponential results. It works in hacking, and it'll work when pursuing life goals. Here's how to do it.

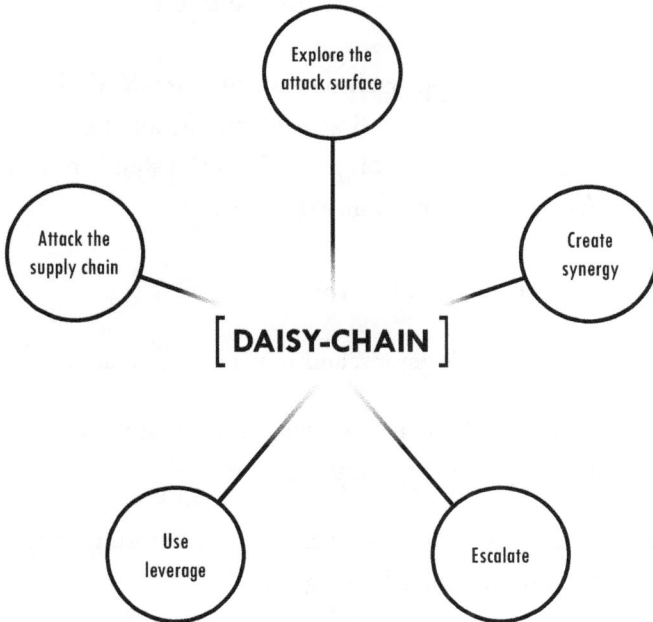

Explore the attack surface

Attack the supply chain

Create synergy

[DAISY-CHAIN]

Use leverage

Escalate

TACTIC #1 Explore the attack surface.
Hackers often combine technical exploits (attacks that leverage vulnerabilities in software) with social engineering (the manipulation of

human behavior). While these channels are distinct—a software vulnerability and a human's cognitive biases don't naturally intersect—hackers creatively combine them to advance attack sequences.

To do that, hackers first identify all the areas of a system that could be attacked, which are collectively known as its *attack surface*. A system's attack surface includes any points where a user (malicious or not) interacts with the system, such as the fields of its login form; its integrations; and even its human elements. Hackers enumerate the discrete parts of the attack surface, probing each one for vulnerabilities. Often, they combine small weaknesses in separate parts of a system's attack surface to create a more significant exploit.

You can apply that approach to your own goals. Before you can combine things, you need to first understand all the possibilities. Start by listing every interaction point of the "system" in which your goal exists. Ask yourself the following questions:

- Who are the key people involved?

- Who makes the decisions, and how are they made?

- What experience, degrees, or certifications are required, and how do people typically obtain them?

- What are the avenues for investing time, effort, money, or other resources in achieving this goal?

- What can be done online versus in person?

- How can I leverage influential people or platforms to reach my goal?

- Are there social media channels or networks that I can utilize?

Be exhaustive. Write down every idea, no matter how small or unconventional. The longer your list, the more options you'll have to explore and combine.

The key is to first map out all potential pathways to your goal. Only then can you identify creative ways to combine them for exponential impact.

TACTIC #2 Create synergy.

Synergy happens when two or more elements interact in a way that amplifies each other's impact, producing a total effect greater than the sum of their individual parts. You might remember the classic high school experiment of mixing baking soda and vinegar. On their own, the substances are stable—one a white powder, the other a clear liquid. But when combined, they create an intense bubbling reaction.

That's synergy: finding elements that work together to create a force multiplier. The key here is making the combination an intentional one. Choose elements that will enhance each other. Not everything pairs well; if you mix dirt with baking soda, nothing happens. For hackers, synergy may mean combining two low-severity vulnerabilities such that they amplify each other's impact, turning two otherwise minor issues into a catastrophic security risk.

You've likely experienced synergy in your career. Pursuing formal education builds skills, while networking creates opportunities. Doing both significantly increases your professional potential. A keynote speaker who is also an author gains credibility, while an author who speaks on stage reaches a broader audience. Time management software helps you track tasks, but pairing it with time blocking transforms your productivity.

As you pursue your goals, don't just add things—combine elements that will strengthen each other to produce an outsized effect.

TACTIC #3 **Escalate.**

Escalation entails sequential progress, with each success building on the previous one. Unlike synergy, which is about *amplification*, escalation is about *momentum*. In hacking, a prime example is privilege escalation: a technique in which an attacker systematically obtains a higher-than-intended level of access within a system. The attacker might start with limited permissions (such as those granted to a standard user account) and then exploit vulnerabilities that move them up the hierarchy of permissions, eventually obtaining full administrative control of the system.

Consider how a tiny spark can grow into a forest fire. A cigarette butt, still smoldering, lands in dry grass. The ember meets fuel, and a flame is ignited. The flame spreads to nearby brush, then to trees, and then to entire neighborhoods. What started as a small ember has transformed into an unstoppable force. That's escalation: turning a small beginning into a massive outcome through a chain reaction of compounding progress.

You see this pattern in business growth as well. It's common for a software company to begin by building only a bare-bones version of its idea, known as a *minimum viable product* (MVP). The purpose of developing an MVP is to test the market without overcommitting your resources. Once a company's MVP has proved its value, the company can tailor its solution to a specific audience and focus on owning its niche. Having gained momentum, it can enhance its branding, build customer loyalty, and expand into adjacent markets and revenue streams. Each step builds on the last. The company's success is built not on isolated wins but on an escalating chain of progress.

That's how you escalate. Turn early traction into exponential success. Start small, let the wins stack up, and build momentum until growth becomes inevitable.

TACTIC #4 Use leverage.

Leverage is the practice of strategically using external resources to achieve far more than you could achieve alone. It's multiplying your results by tapping into outside forces such as money, people, technology, or resources.

In finance, *leverage* refers to the practice of borrowing money to amplify your returns. For example, a real estate investor might buy a $1 million residential property with just $250,000 in cash, borrowing the rest from a bank. Over time, the property would generate income and appreciate in value while its tenants paid off the bank loan. Assuming an annual growth rate of 4 percent (the average annual growth rate of US residential real estate over the past 100 plus years),[45] in 30 years, that $1 million property would be worth more than $3.25 million. A $3.25 million property purchased for $250,000? That's the power of leverage! Multiply your results by effectively combining resources.

Hackers frequently use leverage to maximize their impact, often by exploiting external resources. For instance, consider denial-of-service (DoS) attacks, which seek to render systems unusable by overwhelming them with requests. To defend against such an attack, you need to shut off that flood of requests.

Think of it like being in a water-gun fight. When one person is squirting you, you just have to stop or evade that one person. However, there is a special kind of DoS attack called a *distributed DoS (DDoS) attack*. Like any DoS attack, a DDoS attack seeks to overwhelm a system in order to render it unusable. The difference is

---

45 According to the S&P CoreLogic Case-Shiller Home Price Index, a widely used benchmark that tracks changes in US single-family home values over time through repeat sales.

that rather than flooding the target system with requests from *one* source, a DDoS attack uses *many* sources. The attacker compromises a series of systems to gain control over their computational power and then uses that accumulated power to overload the target system. Defending against that kind of attack is much, much harder. It's like being in that water-gun fight, but rather than trying to avoid getting soaked by one person, you're contending with fifty people. Even if you're able to dodge one or two of them, it'll be pretty hard to not get soaked by the rest.

You'll want to approach your goals as though you're launching a DDoS attack. Attack them from as many angles as possible, leveraging as many resources as possible. A classic nontechnical example of this idea is asking multiple people to refer or recommend you for something. When you are trying to impress a decision maker on your own, they might blow you off. However, if they hear about your merits from many people across different aspects of their lives—people they trust or respect—you become pretty hard to ignore. That's leverage.

You can apply the same principle to your goals by using external resources to scale your efforts.

First, collaborate with mentors or experts who can offer insights and connections that would otherwise be inaccessible to you.

Second, leverage software or platforms that enable you to automate tasks or enhance your efficiency.

Third, seek partnerships or alliances with individuals or organizations whose goals align with yours so that you can share resources and mutually benefit from one another's strengths.

By creatively combining resources, you can significantly amplify your results and more effectively achieve your goals.

TACTIC #5 Attack the supply chain.

Hackers love to find supply chain weaknesses. In cybersecurity, a "supply chain" includes all the entities involved in the production, distribution, and maintenance of software or hardware, such as suppliers, vendors, service providers, and other third parties. Attackers love to focus on the components of a supply chain because each one has the potential to become a vulnerable point of attack. By targeting the weaker links in a supply chain, a hacker can compromise the primary target, executing a tactic known as a *supply chain attack*.

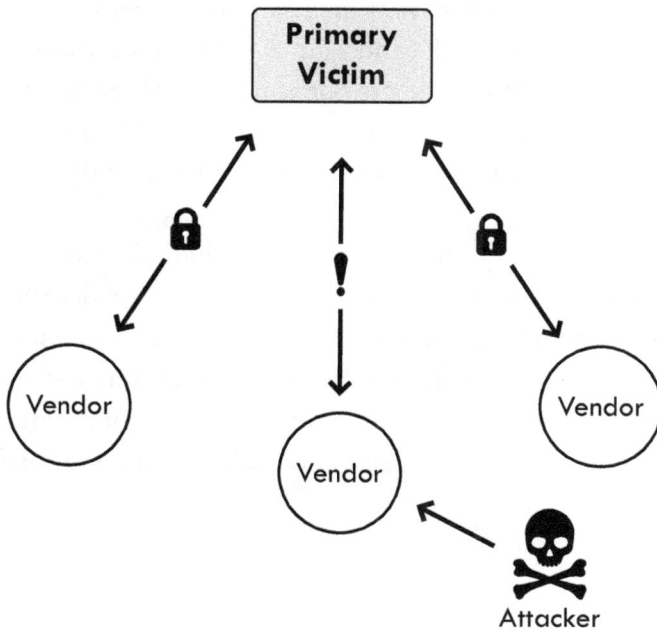

In supply chain attacks, hackers might insert malicious code into software during its development, tamper with hardware components, or exploit vulnerabilities in third-party services. Their goal is typically to gain unauthorized access to the primary target or to distribute malware through trusted channels.[46]

One famous example is the breach of retail giant Target. Attackers compromised Target's air-conditioning service vendor and leveraged the vendor's privileged access to move laterally through Target's network. Eventually, they accessed its payment systems and stole millions of customers' credit card data.

A supply chain attack is distinct from daisy chaining; the former involves compromising a primary target by attacking weaker parties, while the latter involves combining multiple vulnerabilities to amplify the attack's outcome. They do have something significant in common, though: Both rely on the relationships between entities.

Every organization depends on a network of third parties. Those parties might include providers of essential services like janitorial work or niche services like localization; advisory boards; or outsourced HR and payroll teams. This interdependence creates opportunities.

When pursuing your own goals, consider the ecosystem of your target. Is there a pathway through one of its dependencies that might provide an advantage? For example, if you're seeking funding for a start-up from a specific investor, can you network your way to success by connecting with the CEO of a company in its portfolio? A warm introduction will likely be far more effective than a cold outreach.

---

46   The chaotic risk landscape of vendors, suppliers, and trusted third parties is so complex and critical to cybersecurity that we at ISE knew we had to build a software solution to address it. If you work at a big company with lots of vendors and are responsible for protecting something valuable, you might want to check out https://startvrm.com.

Viewing your goal as part of a larger ecosystem rather than a stand-alone target will reveal additional opportunities to combine things in ways that exponentially increase the impact of your efforts.

QUICK RECAP

► Creative combinations produce exponential results.

► To daisy-chain is to combine multiple weaknesses that may not be that useful on their own but deliver exponential impact when combined.

► Implement the following tactics: explore the attack surface, create synergy, escalate, use leverage, and attack the supply chain.

For templates, exercises, and other tools to help you apply this, visit https://tedharrington.com/more.

Now that you've learned how to combine ideas for exponential impact, it's time to take that thinking to places most people wouldn't dare go.

CHAPTER 11

ATTEMPT THE ABNORMAL

Nonstandard approaches lead to
unexpected breakthroughs.

"You can't access it if you don't have permission."

He wasn't wrong. Nor was he right.

Our team was meeting with a new client in preparation for a security assessment of its software system. The company's CTO was explaining the access controls of the system, which was used by movie studios in the production process.

If there is one type of company that cares *a lot* about the security of its digital assets, it is movie studios. To be allowed to work on upcoming blockbuster films, our client needed to prove that its system was resistant to attack.

As the CTO explained how the system worked, what it protected, and how, we came to the topic of permissions. The system was set up such that a user with access to one title (let's say a blockbuster movie about aliens) would not have access to other titles (such as, say, a blockbuster movie about superheroes).

Our mission was to explore whether that was the case. Were users in fact prevented from accessing content that should've been inaccessible to them?

As we began the security assessment, it became clear that the system worked as intended. A normal user could not access content that they did not have permission to access.

At least it seemed that way at first. But we weren't done.

As you've learned by now, hackers don't give up easily. We had verified that the *standard* way of gaining unauthorized access—trying to open other content by navigating the user interface—didn't work. Then it was time to explore some *nonstandard* ways. That's the essence of hacking: creatively exploring the abnormal, unknown, overlooked ways of thinking about a problem.

As we explored how the system worked, we realized that projects were numbered sequentially. That meant we could enumerate all projects: We could look at the ID number of the project we *did* have access to and increase it by one to identify that of the next project.

When we attempted to access additional projects by using sequential ID numbers, it turned out that the technique alone wasn't enough. However, we noticed that the system responded differently if a project existed than if it didn't. That meant that the system was showing us which project IDs were associated with valid existing projects (and which were not).

We couldn't yet exploit the system, but that discovery helped us further a potential attack scenario. We were making progress.

Next, we looked at an existing feature of the system that enabled users to create offline backups of their projects. That's where things got exciting. Could we create a backup of a project we didn't have access to?

Sure enough, as long as we knew the ID of a project, the system would allow us to create a backup of it. Once we had the backup, *we could open it.* That meant we could duplicate and then access any project, including projects we weren't allowed to access. It worked for every single movie in the system. We could access every single detail, including the content itself.

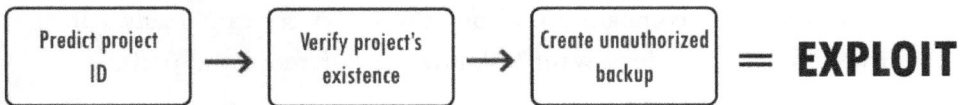

Predict project ID → Verify project's existence → Create unauthorized backup = **EXPLOIT**

That was the worst-case scenario. If an attacker could access a studio's valuable content before its theatrical release, it could destroy the movie's box office revenue. Attacks like that are financial catastrophes for movie studios, which invest millions of dollars (even hundreds of millions) in productions and make most of their profits on movies within a few weeks of their theatrical releases. If a movie is leaked first, that money might never appear.

I love that attack sequence because it's a vivid demonstration of hackers' creativity. We confirmed that the system prevented unauthorized access *when used as intended.* But that's the thing about hackers: *They find another way.*

That different way is often unusual, unexpected, and *creative*.

We combined multiple flaws in the system and abused existing functionality. As a result, we found a way to access things we weren't allowed to access.

We advised our client on the severity of the issue and how to fix it. The company did, and then we verified that the solution worked (a process known as *remediation testing*). We then supplied it with a report to share with its customers. The report proved the company's commitment to security, earning it the trust of major studios. That translated into lucrative contracts for years to come.

There is a disappointing trend among certain companies in the security world: selling ineffective, lightweight, low-effort *scans* as though they were proper thorough, rigorous *security assessments*— even when the companies selling them know that they are not. Furthermore, most companies that buy those services can't really tell the difference (or don't want to know the difference and prefer to just buy what is cheap).

Our client wanted an assessment that would go further than a cheap scan, which would not have been able to find the types of issues we discovered. That decision to be thorough sent a clear message to its movie studio customers about the company's priorities—that it was willing to invest real effort into protecting their most valuable content. That commitment resonated with the company's customers and ultimately led to wonderful outcomes for the business.

By making that choice, the company opened the door for deeper testing. That gave us the opportunity to apply the hacker mindset—to go beyond standard checks and creatively explore the system. In doing so, we uncovered unexpected flaws that, once fixed, enabled the client to earn the trust of major studios and secure long-term revenue.

Observing This Mindset in the Real World

If you've ever presented to a company's board of directors, you know that it can be difficult—especially if you're asking the board to spend money on something as intangible as cybersecurity.

Ensuring security has become crucial for board directors. Getting hacked wreaks havoc on a company's operations. It's expensive to respond to an incident. It's expensive to try to prevent it from happening again—and often unclear where or how to invest to do that effectively. A company's stock price usually plummets after a security breach and takes a long time to recover (if it does at all). Sometimes board members get fired after a security breach.

Given all that, you'd think that presenting to the board about security should be easy.

It is not.

I know a chief information security officer (CISO) who found that out the hard way.

She was leading the security program at a public company—her first time in a CISO role—and preparing to ask the board to fund a large security initiative. As the meeting neared, she developed a presentation that was clear, concise, and actionable. The initiative would deliver meaningful change. It was going to be an easy win.

However, something unexpected happened.

On the day of the presentation, she encountered tremendous opposition. She got absolutely hammered with questions, some of which felt borderline accusatory. She didn't feel attacked, but she definitely didn't feel supported, either. Despite all her preparation, the board rejected her proposal.

She left the meeting bewildered. The company needed this security initiative. She'd made a strong case backed by data and clear, quantifiable outcomes. Yet the board wanted absolutely nothing to do with it. What had happened?

CISOs commonly face that kind of resistance. Few board members come from the security profession themselves, so they usually don't understand it from the inside. Security is hard to understand, much less measure. It tends to be viewed as an expensive cost center, and it's certainly not seen as a driver of profit.[47]

Many CISOs simply must accept that this is how it goes (at least sometimes). You present the case. The board doesn't quite understand or agree with it. You go back to work with less funding than you need (or none at all). That's the standard path.

But she refused to accept that reality. The standard approach had failed—it was time to try something else.

In the days that followed, she reflected on what had gone wrong and realized her mistake.

She had relied on logic and data when the situation had instead required human connection. She'd been in a room where clarity mattered—but influence mattered more. She had optimized for precision, not persuasion.

Determined to try again, she decided to learn more about each board member. She wanted to understand each board member's perspective, motivations, and approach to decision-making. But there was a problem: Most of them were too busy to meet with her. Instead of giving up, she focused on the one board member she already knew. She persisted until he agreed to meet with her. During that meeting, she spent more time listening than speaking. She learned what motivated him and reframed her case to align with his priorities. By the end of the meeting, he was fully on board.

---

47 These views are wrong, by the way. Security delivers a competitive advantage that translates into profit. If you want to learn more about that, read *Hackable*.

She then asked for his help with securing time with another board member, which he happily gave. When she met with that board member, my friend won her over too and asked for her help with setting up the next meeting. Then she repeated the process until she had successfully met with all of them. One by one, she won them over.

When the next board meeting arrived, she nailed it. She knew what each of them cared about and how each one made decisions. She understood what message to deliver and how to deliver it.

Less than a year after that first failed attempt, she got the board to approve her critical security initiative.

She's gone on to be one of the most successful CISOs I know. She now serves on boards herself in addition to fulfilling her CISO duties.

She didn't give up. She got creative. The standard approach was to present logic backed by data and to expect her idea to be approved on its objective merits. That failed. The creative nonstandard way was to lobby individuals, build social proof, and reframe her message in a way that ensured it would be heard.

She found another pathway. That's creativity: rethinking the usual approach and then doing something unexpected that actually works.

That's what you'll want to do, too.

How to Apply This to Your Life

Pursuing abnormal, nonstandard approaches can be challenging because it requires you to explore the unknown. However, there are a number of tactics you can implement to help you break free from conventional approaches. Here are a few.

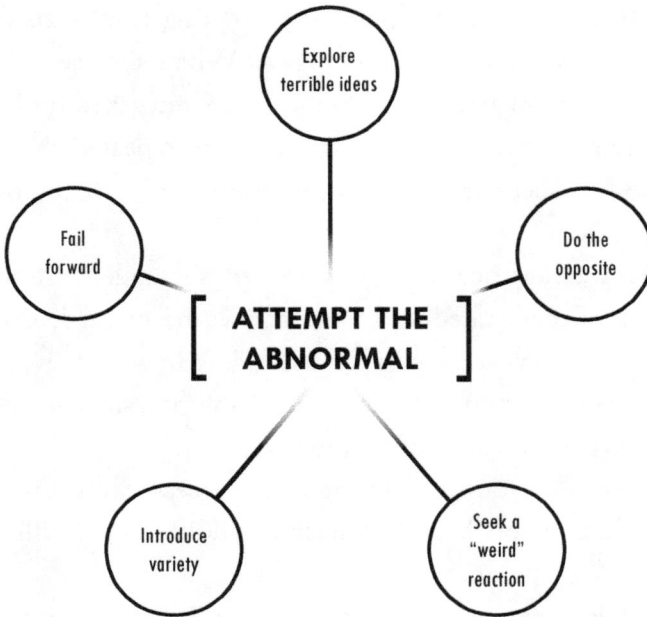

TACTIC #1 **Explore terrible ideas.**

Hackers are constantly trying things that don't work. It's part of the process. They know the path to a good idea usually runs through a field of bad ones. The cool thing about bad ideas is that they usually have the seed of a good idea buried inside them. When bad ideas present themselves, you'll want to explore them. Exploration stimulates creativity.

My favorite conversations with Steve always begin with "Here's a terrible idea..." Whenever one of us utters that phrase, it *always* gets the other person excited. We know that it will stretch our creative thinking and lead us to good ideas. We skip the part that most people start with: rejecting a bad idea for the obvious reasons that make it a bad idea. We openly explore the bad idea without making an initial judgment.

We aren't oblivious; we can clearly see what makes a bad idea *bad*. But we don't let that stop the creative process. We ignore the parts of an idea that make it terrible and focus instead on the seeds that could lead to good ideas. We then expand on those good parts, exploring how we can effectively capitalize on them.

I once heard that when writing what would become the legendary film *Good Will Hunting*, Ben Affleck said to Matt Damon, "Don't judge me for how bad my bad ideas are; judge me for how good my good ideas are." When I came across that, I thought to myself, "HACKER!" *That* is the hacker ethos.

When you judge and impose limitations on yourself, you hold yourself back. If you're holding yourself back, you'll never—and I mean *never*—be able to find a different pathway to your goal. So relax. Let the bad ideas come and go. Considering bad ideas actually stimulates creativity. Explore the ideas and see where they take you. They'll probably lead you to a new way of tackling your goal.

TACTIC #2 Do the opposite.

I mean this in the most literal way possible: Consider how most people would approach a situation, and then do the exact opposite.

Hackers are masters of exploring the opposite. That is how hackers find the overlooked shortcuts that everyone else has missed. It's how they find different pathways to exploitable security vulnerabilities that others thought did not exist. At ISE, when we meet with clients, they often walk us through how their tech works with something like "It goes A, then B, then C." When our hackers hear that, they immediately explore what would happen if they just did C first. It doesn't always work, but you'd be surprised by how often it does. Even when it doesn't work, the exercise exposes new ways of thinking about the tech, how it works, and how to break it.

You can apply that highly creative process to your own goal, too. Here's how.

First, identify the goal.

Second, list out all of the ways that people normally approach the goal.

Third, for each of those, write down whatever the opposite would be. Explore whether any steps can be done in a different order, for example. If so, what might the effect be? How could it be used to your advantage?

Fourth, evaluate the merits of each opposite approach. What conditions would need to exist for it to work? How can you create those conditions?

Fifth, try one of those opposites.

Sixth, measure the results.

Seventh, try another one.

Eighth, repeat.

There is creative magic in being different, so try doing the opposite of what everyone else is and see what happens.

TACTIC #3 Seek a "weird" reaction.

Much of hacking is about feedback loops: probing a system, observing how it reacts, and then using that feedback to further your efforts. Most of the time, a system behaves the way you'd expect it to. Things get exciting for hackers when a system does something weird, unusual, or unexpected, because it tells them that there might be a flaw in the aspect of the system they're investigating. It encourages further exploration. It leads them to ask what caused the unexpected behavior. What underlying assumptions may have led to it? Are those assumptions flawed? Are those assumptions repeated elsewhere?

Hackers seek out unexpected behavior, error messages, and failure states because they are information gold mines. A system working as intended doesn't reveal much, but when a system breaks, it often exposes valuable insights. A failure can directly disclose useful information, reveal flaws in the system's logic, or even create new avenues for further exploration. Discovering how a system fails often leads to exciting opportunities.

As you pursue your goal, you're going to expect things to unfold in a certain way. Pay special attention when they do not unfold in that way. Take notice when there's a blip in a process and things unfold slightly differently than expected. Test the process in ways that could force an unusual reaction.

Those abnormalities are the areas where you might be able to find a new unexpected pathway. It might be a route that no one else has thought to travel before. That pathway may save you time, effort, or resources. On that pathway, you may have little or no competition. Pay attention to what you *think* is supposed to happen, try to find the moments when things get *weird*, and then pursue those weird threads as far as you can. Here's how.

First, define what "normal" looks like. Start by understanding what the typical process should be. Take note of what you expect at each step. Having a clear picture of "normal" first will help you recognize anomalies as they arise.

Second, experiment to provoke weird reactions. Don't *wait* for something unusual to happen—try to force it. Ask yourself the following:

- What if I skip a step or reverse the order of the steps?

- What if I push the limits of what's allowed?

- How can I misuse this process?

- How can it help me bypass a roadblock, limitation, or obstacle?

Approach this experiment with curiosity and without fear of failure. Weird reactions are the goal, so anything unusual is a win.

Third, document the unexpected. When you notice something weird, write down exactly what happened, why it felt unexpected, and what you think might have caused it. The details will help you find the root of the anomaly in the next step.

Fourth, ask probing questions. Once you've identified an unusual reaction, start breaking it down:

- What caused this behavior?

- Was it the result of a flawed assumption in the process or system?

- Does its cause exist in other parts of the system?

- How can I leverage this behavior or turn it into an advantage?

The goal is to understand whether the weirdness represents a unique opportunity that you can use to your advantage.

Finally, evaluate the potential pathway. Ask yourself the following:

- Can this be turned into a shortcut or a new approach?

- Is it scalable or repeatable?

- Does it save me time, effort, or resources?

- Does it offer an advantage that others might not recognize?

Not every anomaly will lead to something valuable, but some will. Those are worth pursuing.

`TACTIC #4` **Introduce variety.**

In the security assessment business, hackers routinely switch between projects. For example, a hacker might take on work for a movie studio in one project, for a fintech firm in the next, and for a healthcare company in the one after that. The variety not only keeps things interesting but also forces hackers into different mental modes. By solving different types of problems, they stretch their thinking, uncover new perspectives, and build on previous learning. A hacker may work on one project, feel stumped, move to a second project, find an interesting exploit chain, and then realize that it's applicable to the first project. Variety ensures not only that hackers remain engaged and excited but also that they continuously find new and creative ways to discover vulnerabilities.

You'll want to do something similar in your own pursuits. Being obsessed with your goal is a good thing, but you'll want to avoid becoming myopic. Variety is the solution.

Variety can come in many forms. You can create variety in your approach, for example, by doing different tasks that still serve the same goal. For instance, if you're starting a company, you'll spend time creating marketing materials like a website. Then you'll switch gears to research potential investors and trends in venture capital. When you return to marketing, you'll have fresh insights from the break and a broader perspective on your overall goal.

Alternatively, you can create variety by doing things that are not related to your goal (at least not on the surface). Pick up a hobby—learn a language, play a sport, or practice an instrument. Although it might not seem like a hobby will help you achieve your goal, I assure you that it will. Giving your brain a break from focusing on your goal and doing something else recharges you, allowing new perspectives to come into focus.

Inspiration strikes me in the most unexpected places. I was recently in Honduras, staying in a rental unit with an air conditioner that I couldn't figure out. It was so bizarre and backward that at first, I was stumped. I just couldn't figure out how it worked. As I was noodling on the logic of the device's operation (or lack thereof), inspiration struck about something completely unrelated: a problem I'd been trying to solve at ISE. There I was, sweating profusely, holding this annoying little remote control in my hand, when suddenly, I solved a difficult business problem that had been plaguing me for weeks. Doing something different enabled me to solve it.

That's the power of variety.

Before we conclude this tactic, let's be careful to differentiate between variety (which is good) and multitasking (which is bad). The two concepts are not the same and should not be confused with each other, so let me be precise: *Multitasking* refers to the performance of more than one task at a time, while *variety* refers to a diversity of experience. Multitasking fractures your attention, leading to errors, lower productivity, and higher stress.[48] Variety, on the other hand, involves alternating between different interests or activities while focusing on only one at a time. Multitasking divides your energy; variety shifts it. Variety creates space for deeper thinking and better results. Seek variety; avoid multitasking.

---

48 There's a massive pile of peer-reviewed psychology studies I could've dropped in here to prove the point. But as I was collecting them all, I realized I was getting sidetracked—chasing an unnecessary distraction to prove something you probably already know from your own lived experience. It would have cost me time, energy, and focus—without meaningfully improving the outcome (and maybe even making it worse). A good little reminder about the perils of multitasking, right there.

TACTIC #6 Fail forward.

One of the things I love about hackers is that they're not deterred by dead ends. In fact, they often find them exciting. They know that if they keep working, thinking, and poking, they'll eventually find a way. The thrill is even greater when they discover something novel; finding a new way to hack a system brings them both pride and joy. It's the ultimate creative journey.

In hacking, as in life, failure is part of the process. As long as it's moving you forward, failure is good. Failure is a teacher. It encourages you to try new things, innovate, and be original. Unfortunately, the word *fail* has become associated with a bad thing, as if a disappointing outcome is defeat. It's not. If an idea doesn't work, you are simply being guided to a different way. Each time a normal, standard way proves unfruitful, the system is telling you to experiment with abnormal, nonstandard ways.

One of the literal definitions of the word *fail* is "to be unsuccessful." What it should really mean is "to be unsuccessful...*so far*." If you were to interrupt a hacker in the middle of a project and learn that they hadn't found any vulnerabilities yet, they wouldn't see it as a failure. They'd tell you they simply hadn't succeeded *yet*. They'd point out the many clues or insights that were bringing them closer to a breakthrough. They'd know that with a little more effort, they'd find a working pathway.

Thinking like that unlocks the ability to try, refine, and try again until you eventually find a way that works. Much of the hacking process is chasing dead ends and red herrings, yet hackers chase them anyway, knowing that each one will move them closer to success. You'll want to do that, too.

Learn from each failure, dead end, or roadblock. Each moment is teaching you something; find out what it is so that you can redirect your efforts toward new unconventional pathways to your goal.

QUICK RECAP

▶ Nonstandard approaches lead to unexpected breakthroughs.

▶ Hackers thrive because there's often a different, unusual way, and they're willing to go find it.

▶ Implement the following tactics: explore terrible ideas, do the opposite, seek a "weird" reaction, introduce variety, and fail forward.

For templates, exercises, and other tools to help you apply this, visit https://tedharrington.com/more.

Hackers are creative, and that ethos drives them to find another way—*especially* if that way is abnormal. Now that you've learned how to apply a hacker's creativity to your life, let's recap all that you've learned in part IV, "Hackers Are Creative." Then we'll jump into the conclusion, where we'll revisit the big ideas from the entire book.

SUMMARY · PART IV

Hackers Are
CREATIVE

| Abuse Functionality | Daisy-Chain | Attempt the Abnormal |

Abuse Functionality

- *Use it differently* to achieve a different outcome.

- *Consider WCPGW* to break out of normal ways of thinking and see a system in a new light.

- *Exploit logic flaws*, because errors in the way a system works can reveal new paths to success.

- *Perform excessive usage testing* to see whether you can overload the system and achieve your goal in an unexpected way.

- *Manipulate parameters*, because minor changes to existing variables can lead you to overlooked pathways.

- *Play with good mischief* to find loopholes, bend expectations, and creatively turn systems on their heads.

Daisy-Chain

- *Explore the attack surface* to identify shortcuts or loopholes.

- *Create synergy* by combining approaches that amplify one another's impact.

- *Escalate* to build unstoppable momentum.

- *Use leverage* to achieve far more than you could on your own.

- *Attack the supply chain* to approach your goal indirectly and capitalize on the larger ecosystem in which your goal exists.

Attempt the Abnormal

- *Explore terrible ideas* as a creative way to find the seeds of good ideas that are buried in bad ones.

- *Do the opposite* to break out of your patterns and find creative new pathways.

- *Seek a "weird" reaction* to uncover the hidden flaws that can help you achieve your goal.

- *Introduce variety* to stimulate creativity.

- *Fail forward* to find the learning opportunities buried within each setback, roadblock, or obstacle.

CONCLUSION

How can something be both hot and cold at the same time?

I pondered that as I looked at my hands, which were glistening with sweat under the harsh lighting of a corporate office lobby. Sweating, yet somehow also icy. What a weird word we have for that: *clammy*.

Do clams sweat?

It was early 2012, and Steve and I had just partnered up to run our security consulting company, ISE. I had set up a meeting with the CTO of a big financial services firm who was interested in possibly hiring us. It was the first big meeting of this new phase of my career. I was nervous, and my mind was spinning.

A lot of my college buddies had wound up in finance, so I knew that finance people tend to dress conservatively and professionally. I figured it would be best for us to wear suits to fit in with the bankers. There were two problems with that, though: Hackers generally dress casually, and Steve dislikes wearing a suit. He once referred to a black-tie wedding as a "costume party" because "wearing a suit is costume enough for me."[49] However, I felt that

---

49 I laughed so hard when I heard this that I told him it deserved to be in a book someday. Well, here we are!

it was important that we dress the way bankers dress in order to build trust with them.

I insisted. Steve relented, and we put on suits.

So there we were, sitting in this beautiful lobby and waiting to meet this important CTO—in our suits. When the CTO came to greet us, two things stood out. First, he was dressed casually, wearing jeans and a hoodie.

Second, he didn't say hello or even introduce himself. He just said, "What's with the suits, guys?"

Steve shot me a look that said, "What the *HELL*, Ted!"

All these years later, that moment still lives in hilarious infamy at our company.

I should have known by then that the path to success is not through conformity.

I had theorized that because bankers wear suits, we should, too. That is the very definition of conformity, and conformity is not your friend. We didn't look like hackers; we looked like pretenders. We were not authentic, and it backfired.

Fast-forward many years to another big meeting. This time, Steve and I were about to pitch a potential investor in our software company, StartVRM. The purpose of the meeting was to ask the company to give us millions of dollars to help grow the business. This time around, however, we chose not to conform. In fact, we exemplified each of the major themes you learned in this book.

We were curious. Before pitching this investor, we studied the company's investing patterns, observed the personalities of the key players, and evaluated trends in the investment market.

We were committed. We spent many months on research, prep, and rapport building.

We were creative. We developed a deal structure that was

unusual in both its terms and its benefits for both parties.

And perhaps above all, we were non-conforming. At a key moment of the pitch, I sent a text to my executive assistant, Lauren.

"Now."

Moments later, she entered the conference room. We'd already run through the entire pitch—the value proposition, the traction, and the ask.

"One last thing," I said as Lauren handed out glass tumblers.

"We know you like scotch, and we do too."

With that, Lauren placed two bottles of eighteen-year-old scotch on the table.

The move was *wildly* non-conforming. Pitch meetings are supposed to be formal, focused on the numbers, and *very serious business*. However, in all those months of curiously studying this investor and the key execs we were dealing with, we'd learned they really liked scotch—and they didn't take themselves too seriously, even in moments like this. So we took a gamble on weaving that into our pitch.

It worked beautifully.

They *loved* it.

After the pitch was over, the lead investor literally said, "This was the best pitch we've ever heard." It wasn't just because of the scotch (though that helped). It was because we approached the deal with curiosity, non-conformity, commitment, and creativity. Those attributes triggered a powerful and positive response from the investor.

Shortly thereafter, we received an investment offer that significantly exceeded market norms. It was an amount of money that would have forever changed the trajectory of our business. The deal ultimately did not close, but the key lesson is clear:

*When you think like a hacker, you unlock the ability
to think differently.*

*Thinking differently reveals new pathways that
others have overlooked.*

*And those pathways will allow you to navigate change,
transform obstacles into opportunities, and achieve your goals.*

Think Beyond the System

Everything in this book boils down to a single simple idea: *Think beyond the system.*

Limiting your thinking to the confines of a system requires you to work within its rules, structure, and logic. When you think *beyond* the system, you look past the system's boundaries. You adopt a mindset of utilizing unconventional methods to bypass its intended design, rules, and expectations. As a result, you discover unconventional methods of problem-solving.

Thinking beyond the system means being willing to break free from convention. It means not limiting yourself to the traditional or well-traveled routes to your goal. It means seeking out innovative, unconventional ways to succeed. It means utilizing strengths and resources that others might overlook or underestimate. It means anticipating obstacles and developing creative strategies for overcoming them.

That is exactly how hackers think. You can think like that, too.

When you think beyond the system, you find new pathways to achieving big, lofty, meaty meaningful goals. It's how you navigate change.

Yes, it is easier said than done. But the good news is that you've learned exactly how to do it.

First, be *curious*. Ask why and figure out how things work.

Second, be *non-conforming*. Challenge assumptions, break the rules, and ask "what if?"

Third, be *committed*. Prioritize passion, persist, and adapt.

Fourth and finally, be *creative*. Abuse functionality, daisy-chain, and attempt the abnormal.

HACKERS are...

Curious
non-Conforming
Committed
Creative

It's difficult, but it *is* achievable. That's the point: *Do* hard things, and you'll *accomplish* hard things.

Hackers know that. Now, you do too.

Everything you've learned in this book is designed to be *used*. Every chapter title is a *verb*. Every key idea is expressed as a *tactic*. This isn't theory—it's a *tool kit*. You can—and should—take action on each idea.

On the following pages is a summary of the actions you can take. Take a picture and send it to your friends or post it on social media. Maybe even rip the pages out of the book so that you can hang them somewhere visible (I'll forgive you).

There's also an appendix that summarizes all of the exercises detailed in this book and tells you where to go to download additional worksheets and templates. Just flip forward a few pages, and you'll find it.

Throughout this book, I've shined the spotlight on hackers. As our time together comes to a close, allow me to turn the spotlight on you now.

You are a hacker.

You Are a Hacker

As you've learned by now, *hacker* doesn't refer only to a person with the technical abilities to find exploitable security vulnerabilities in software systems. Hacking isn't about *computers*; it's about *life*.

A hacker is a curious, non-conforming, committed, creative problem solver.

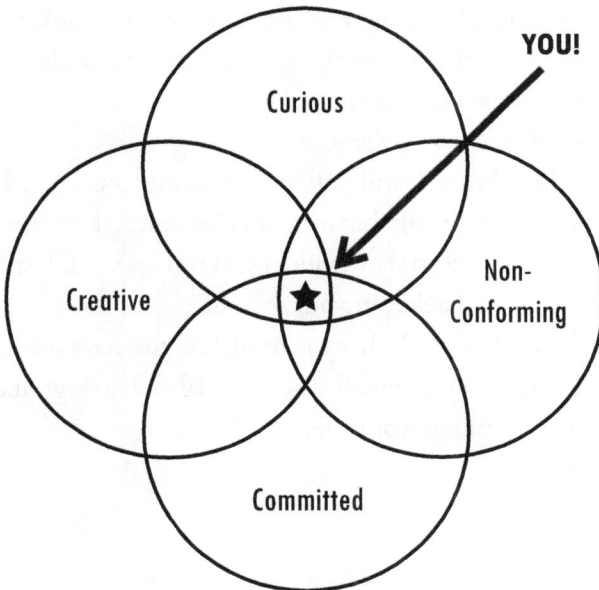

You've read this entire book, which tells us something about you, too: You are probably all of those things.

So I want you to do something. This is not for me; it's for you. It's going to feel silly, and you've probably never done it before. That's okay. Remember: Hackers give themselves permission to think and behave differently.

I want you to say the following out loud, right now:

"I am a hacker!"

Seriously.

Stop reading. Put the book down for a moment. Say those words out loud.

"I AM A HACKER!"

Feels good, doesn't it?

This isn't some absurd hippie bullshit. You *are* a hacker.

You're the kind of person who reads an entire book to learn a new paradigm so that you can navigate change, turn obstacles into opportunities, and achieve your goals.

That is exactly what a hacker does.

You've looked inward and found your inner hacker. Now give yourself permission to bring that inner hacker *out*. Ask yourself, What would a hacker do? Go apply the ideas you just learned. Explore, fail, adapt, try again. Be a hacker in your own life.

You now have all the tools that you need. You also have me as a friend and a resource (I'm only an email away at ted@tedharrington.com).

It's time to go change your life.

You got this.

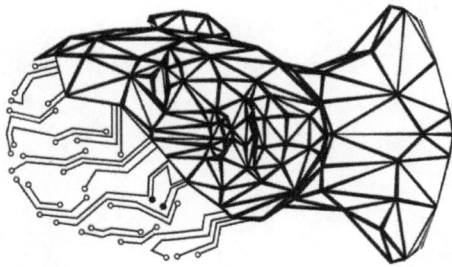

INNER HACKER
A NEW WAY OF THINKING

01 Ask "Why?"

Go deeper with "The 5 Whys"
Determine the purpose of the system
Analyze a different viewpoint
Look at past performance
Deliver your questions with care
Know when to stop digging

02 Figure Out How It Works

Gather OSINT
Ask open-ended questions
Explore cause and effect
Develop a system map
Reverse-engineer the outcome
Be skeptical

03 Challenge Assumptions

Ask other people
Listen to understand
Test absolutes
Reflect
Stress test
Reject norms
Make it a lifetime practice

04 Break the Rules

Understand the purpose of the rule
Evaluate the effectiveness of the rule
Determine whether the rule is worth breaking
Consider the consequences of breaking the rule
Test the rule (within boundaries)
Advocate for change

05 Ask "What If?"

Give yourself permission
Take risks
Do it often
Implement the principle of least privilege
Accept the negative reactions

06 Prioritize Passion

Teach something
Chase passion outside of your job
Pay out of pocket

07 Persist

Establish self-discipline through habits
Break it into smaller pieces
Love the challenge
Overcome imposter syndrome
Feel the fear and do it anyway
Do one more
Fix your vulnerabilities

08 Adapt

Adjust as you go
Tune in to your instincts
Let the obstacles guide you
Use the scientific method

09 Abuse Functionality

Use it differently
Consider WCPGW
Exploit logic flaws
Perform excessive usage testing
Manipulate parameters
Play with good mischief

10 Daisy-Chain

Explore the attack surface
Create synergy
Escalate
Use leverage
Attack the supply chain

11 Attempt the Abnormal

Explore terrible ideas
Do the opposite
Seek a "weird" reaction
Introduce variety
Fail forward

Learn more at **https://tedharrington.com/more**

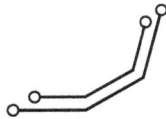

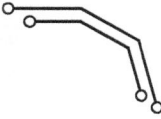

PSST...DID YOU NOTICE THE EASTER EGG?!

◆ ◆ ◆

Hackers combine things in creative ways to unlock unexpected results.

Try it yourself: If you have a copy of *Hackable*, place it side by side with *Inner Hacker*. You might discover a surprise in the combined cover art, revealed only because you gave yourself permission to think like a hacker.

I hope you had as much fun discovering this little Easter egg as I had creating it. It took several years—and two entire books—to bring it to life.

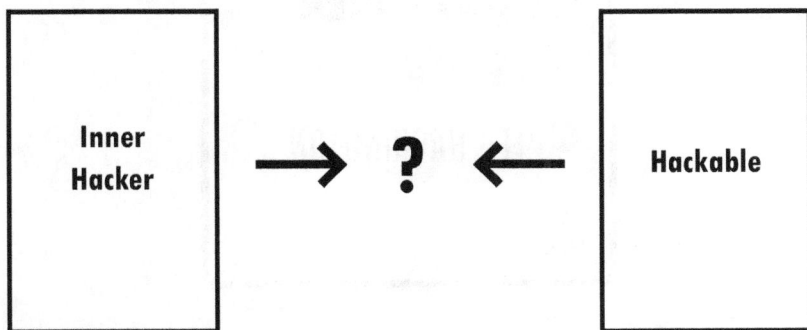

| Inner Hacker | → ? ← | Hackable |

FURTHER READING

Do you want to dive deeper into the hacker mindset and apply it to building better more secure software systems? If you're a CTO, executive, security practitioner, or software developer, *Hackable* is for you.

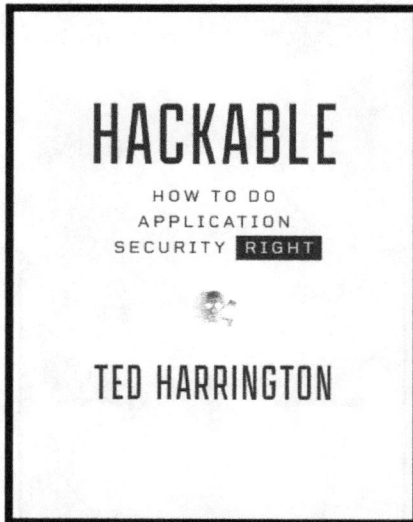

HACKABLE

HOW TO DO
APPLICATION
SECURITY RIGHT

TED HARRINGTON

Available wherever books are sold, in hardcover, paperback, ebook, and audiobook formats.

APPENDIX:
SUMMARY OF ADDITIONAL MATERIAL

You've just read a book about how to think differently. Now it's time to do something with the concepts you've learned.

I've created a set of downloadable tools—worksheets, templates, group exercises, and guides—that will help you put these ideas into action. Each one corresponds to a tactic from the book and gives you a step-by-step way to apply it in your own life.

You can download the full set at https://tedharrington.com/more.

Here's a breakdown of what you'll get—and how each tool will help you:

1. **The Inner Hacker Cheat Sheet**
   Organize everything you've learned about the hacker mindset in one place for quick reference and clarity.

2. **Go Deeper with "The 5 Whys"**
   Bypass surface-level understanding to arrive at deeper meaning by asking why five times in a structured way.

3. **Analyze a Different Viewpoint**
   Understand someone else's reasoning so you can find flaws, assumptions, or strategic advantages in their thinking.

4. **Deliver Your Questions with Care**
   Frame your questions with curiosity rather than criticism to encourage openness and avoid defensiveness.

5. **Explore Cause and Effect**
   Map potential actions to their outcomes to better understand how your choices influence results.

6. **Reverse-Engineer the Outcome**
   Deconstruct the process behind a desired result so that you can replicate or improve on it.

7. **Be Skeptical**
   Strengthen your curiosity by questioning claims, pulling on threads, and probing systems more deeply.

8. **Test Absolutes**
   Find exceptions to absolute statements to uncover hidden assumptions or opportunities.

9. **Reflect**
   Use guided prompts to examine how your thoughts shape your behavior—and how to change them.

10. **Stress Test**
    Spot and question the hidden beliefs that may be limiting your progress.

11. **Reject Norms**
    Consciously resist expectations or conventions that don't serve your goals.

12. **Evaluate the Effectiveness of the Rule**
    Determine whether a rule actually accomplishes what it's supposed to before deciding whether to follow it.

13. Determine Whether the Rule Is Worth Breaking
Wisely utilize your energy by identifying which rules would lead to the biggest breakthroughs if broken.

14. Test the Rule (Within Boundaries)
Experiment with breaking a rule in a way that's safe and ethical so that you can learn from the results.

15. Establish Self-Discipline Through Habits
Build small sustainable habits that increase your capacity to follow through—especially when things get hard.

16. Break It Into Smaller Pieces
Deconstruct large goals into manageable steps so that you can make steady progress without getting overwhelmed.

17. Overcome Imposter Syndrome
Recognize patterns of self-doubt and use reframing techniques to stay grounded in your strengths.

18. Feel the Fear and Do It Anyway
Name your fears, shrink them down to size, and take bold action anyway.

19. Adjust as You Go
Practice mental flexibility so that you can adapt quickly when plans or conditions change.

20. Use a Decision Quadrant
Weigh the pros and cons of action versus inaction to clarify your gut instinct and inform your next move.

21. Make a "Draft Decision"
Try on a temporary decision and evaluate how it feels before committing fully.

22. Use the Scientific Method

Test your ideas systematically so that you can iterate toward success with confidence.

23. Use It Differently

Repurpose a tool, idea, or resource in a creative way to find unexpected solutions.

24. Consider WCPGW

Ask "What could possibly go wrong?" to identify over-looked risks—and playful possibilities.

25. Exploit Logic Flaws

Spot breaks in reasoning that others have missed and turn them into strategic advantages.

26. Play with Good Mischief

Use playful, creative subversion to unlock new pathways.

27. Explore the Attack Surface

Identify every potential point of entry into a system so that you can find unconventional routes to your goal.

28. Use Leverage

Achieve greater results with less effort by using external tools, people, or systems strategically.

29. Do the Opposite

Flip conventional thinking by asking what everyone else would do—and then doing the reverse.

30. Seek a "Weird" Reaction

Trigger unexpected outcomes in a system and use them to uncover hidden opportunities.

ACKNOWLEDGMENTS

Rachael Tubbs.

I considered simply ending this entire section there. Two words. *Rachael. Tubbs.*

I do have many other people to thank, though, so I won't stop there after all. But the fact that I even considered it says everything you need to know about how important you were to this project. This book simply would not exist without you. You guided me through every single phase from inception to editorial, production, and launch. You supported me when I doubted myself, course corrected me when I was off base, called me out on my (seemingly endless) bullshit, and, fortunately, told me when I was on the right track.

This book is for and about the amazing people I've worked alongside at ISE, both current and former. You inspire me every day, not only because of what you *achieve* but also because of how you *think*. I'm in awe of who you are as people: smart, kind, funny, interested, interesting, compassionate, curious, humble, and so much more. Getting to lead a team like ours is truly one of the great blessings of my life.

TJ Preyear, Joel St. John, Chris Vinecombe, Ali Esparza, James Zeits, and Flake Redmond: You gave me incredible stories to use, helped edit the manuscript where needed, and just generally helped me bring the hacker ethos to life. Kyle Perkins, Mickey Bayo,

Mitchell Cooper, John Gleason, Caroline Sullivan, Ben Schmerler, Katie Pickrell, and Bri Bos: You all contributed meaningfully to brainstorming discussions and helped shape my thinking and the direction of the manuscript.

Adam Lennon, you scratched your designer itch and produced the incredible, beautiful interior graphics and layout that gave this book the polish it deserves. Jolene Sundstrom, your editorial support ensured that I said what I meant to say in the tone I meant to say it in without grammatical error. Lauren Quinn, you helped me figure out a publishing model that would work for our goals (and you kept my life on track for many years). Luke Phillips, you helped coordinate the busy schedules of our hackers. Paul Yun, you taught me about hacking cameras. Josh Meyer, you taught me about hacking toilets. Sanjana Sarda, your research on dating apps has become a staple of my keynotes.

And, of course, Steve.

I have a vivid memory of first meeting you—of sitting at the iconic Owl Bar in Baltimore, enshrined in ornate mahogany woodwork and glowing stained-glass windows, with heavy tumblers of whiskey in our hands. Thinking back on that moment, I remember two thoughts that occurred to me. First, *this guy is smart*. And then, much more importantly, *I like this guy*. You've been one of the few constants in my life, which feels like it's always shifting. You've stood by me through my darkest moments and cheered me on in my brightest. You've cared about me not just as a professional but as a human being. When imposter syndrome crept in—when I doubted whether I truly belonged in a world full of computer scientists— you made me feel seen, valued, and smart. Your steady belief in me has been one of the quiet forces shaping my journey, and for that, I am endlessly grateful. Building ISE with you has been one of the greatest honors of my life. Thank you for all the ways you've made me, and everyone else at ISE, better. Thank you for being my friend.

I interviewed many people for this project, including some of the most prominent voices in the hacker community. Thank you, Chris Roberts, John Hammond, Casey Ellis, Phillip Wylie, Naomi Buckwalter, Beau Woods, Jason Haddix, Deral Heiland, Terry Dunlap, Don Donzal, Bryson Bort, Justin "Hutch" Hutchinson, Chloé Messdaghi, Barret Darnell, and Nicole Little. You directly shaped the insights in this book and helped me understand what it means to be a hacker. Your perspective guided me past the flat, literal definition of the term and helped me see the concept in all its dimensions—full of light, shape, and meaning. Rinki Sethi, you provided an invaluable perspective on the business challenges security leaders face. Michael Kuehner, you gave me the viewpoint of an attorney (and an independent thinker), helping me understand rules and rule breaking.

To the team at TEDxFrankfurt—this book is a direct result of your decision to put me on your stage. After my talk, as I stood beside some copies of *Hackable*, an attendee breathlessly asked me whether the book would teach her the hacker mindset I had just spoken about. I told her that it sort of would but that it was more about securing software systems. She was crestfallen. She paused and then asked a question that would change the trajectory of my life.

"Well, can you write that book?"

That question led to the one you're holding in your hands.

Giving a TED Talk was a lifelong dream of mine, and getting to do so in such an amazing city was spectacular. But even more than that, getting to do it *with* and *for* such incredible people was a gift. Thanks to Carla Banc, Tamara Laudt, Mohammed Mishal, Eda Sahinkaya, Erisa Behluli, Viktoria Albrecht, Oliver Viplove, and the rest of the amazing team for inviting me into your world. Thank you, Rhea Whessel, for pushing me to turn my original idea into one worthy of a global TED audience.

Sarah Birmingham, first of all, I love you. Second, thank you for making the cover of this book as badass as it is. Ignore the noise: People *absolutely should* judge a book by its cover. I just hope the content lives up to the promise you made with its design. I'm lucky to be your cousin, but even if we weren't related, I'd still choose you as a friend. Fortunately for me, I get *both*. Our bond means the world to me, and I'm grateful for it and for you.

To those of you who publicly backed this project and provided inspiring testimonials—thank you. Eli Mezei, Jeff Civillico, Casey Ellis, Carla Banc, and Theresa Payton: You are each legends in your own way, and your support is the gasoline that will fuel the fire I hope to spark with the ideas in this book.

People rarely talk about how *writing* a book is mostly about *editing* a book. I wrote the first draft of this in two months and then spent two *years* editing it. The ideas it contains today are pretty similar to those in that first, very bad, draft, except now they're clear, concise, relatable, understandable, implementable, and actually worth reading. I couldn't have done that alone. Thank you to my editorial team, especially Brannan Sirratt. You were more than an editor. You were a friend, a therapist, and a copilot helping me bring this idea to life. Thank you to the many ISE folks who edited the manuscript along the way, including Rachael, TJ, Joel, Chris, Ali, James, and Jolene.

Writing a book can be a lonely journey. Not for me. I'm grateful to have found my *Scribe Fam*, a tribe of fellow authors who helped bring *Hackable* to life and continue to support me to this day. One in particular stands out: Ron Thurston. Ron, you're one of the few people I can talk to about business, writing, life, and tech (and then life again) all in one conversation. I've learned so much from you, and I deeply value your friendship. As you released your second book just ahead of mine,

I got to follow your lead through each stage, learning from both your mindset and your moves. Thank you for showing me the way.

Elena, your impact on this book—and on me—has been profound. You've shown a kind of patience I didn't know was possible. Your quiet, steady support became part of the foundation I built this book on. You show up in ways both big and small, and every "I'm proud of you" has meant more than I can explain. Thank you for standing by me and for believing in me—even in the moments when I doubted myself.

Mom and Dad, I dedicated my first book, *Hackable*, to you because the life you created for me made it possible to do hard things that matter in the service of other people. I'm a grown-ass man now, and yet I still work every day to try to make you proud. That's a powerful driver for me. It fueled my desire to write a second book—and the grit it took to see it through. Thank you for all the ways you've loved and supported me. It's because of you that I get to put work like this into the world.

Finally, thank you to everyone who read this book—including *you*. Yes, you, with this book in your hands right now. The kind of person who would read an entire book (even the acknowledgments!) in pursuit of a new paradigm is the kind of person who's always working to grow. Curious people change the world. If I haven't met you in person yet, I hope I someday will.

Every person mentioned here made this book better. You've made *me* better. There are many people named in these pages whom I love deeply, even if I didn't say it directly. Please know it's true. Your involvement will help all who consume the ideas in these pages.

I'm eternally grateful to all of you.

Happy hacking,

Ted

ABOUT THE AUTHOR

◆ ◆ ◆

Ted Harrington is the #1 bestselling author of *Hackable*, which led to his TED Talk, "Why You Need to Think Like a Hacker." He's the Executive Partner at Independent Security Evaluators (ISE)—a company of ethical hackers famous for hacking cars, medical devices, and web applications—and co-founder of StartVRM, a software platform that simplifies vendor risk management. Their clients include Google, Amazon, and Netflix, and their work has been featured in more than 100 media outlets, including *The New York Times*, *The Wall Street Journal*, the *Financial Times*, and *Forbes*. He co-founded IoT Village, a hacking competition that has produced four DEF CON Black Badge winners.

To get help with security testing or vendor risk management—or to book Ted as a keynote speaker—visit **tedharrington.com**.

www.ingramcontent.com/pod-product-compliance
Lightning Source LLC
Chambersburg PA
CBHW051723260326
41914CB00031B/1706/J